Wonderment

by Isabella Clarence

This book is a work of non-fiction based on the life, experiences and recollections of the author. Some names have been changed in this book to protect the privacy of the individuals involved.

No part of this book may be reproduced, stored in a retrieval system, or transmitted in any form or by any means, electronic, mechanical, photocopying, recording or otherwise, without express written permission of the author.

www.isabellaclarence.co.uk

ISBN-9781673506402

CONTENTS

ACKNOWLEDGMENTS

What a lovely way to be able to start a book by simply using the words, 'thank you.'

Thank you Jean for writing the foreword to this book. Now you're bound to ask: who's Jean?

If you read my first two books you will have come across Jean on more than one occasion.

She was the close friend I turned to in 1988 when my father passed this life and I heard his voice from the spirit world for the first time. It was Jean I turned to when my writing of messages down from the Spirit world began in earnest. It was Jean who supported me and listened to me when other friends would have run a mile if I'd tried to explain to them what was happening to me. I can never thank her enough for the support and love she gave me at that time in my life. She was the only person outside of our family that I gave a copy of my father's poems to in 1989. And I know she still has that file after all these years. It was for that very reason that I felt she was the perfect choice to ask to write the forward to this first book of poems.

Not only did Jean kindly write the forward, her own wonderful words are also going to end this book.

And that for me is perfect.

Now, I would like to say a huge thank you to all the other dear Souls who helped me produce this book.

Without the love of our loved ones who are now in Heaven, this book would never have come into existence. It is with a very grateful heart that I say thank you to each and every one of you, especially to my father.

Next, to my beautiful daughter who once again edited her mothers work and, yes, I got lots of; rewrite – move – No – what the... – move this to another chapter – does not follow – not sure about this! – do you have permission? – eh! – why?

– muddled – not needed – and so much more, but we

got there. Thank you my precious girl. You have done another fantastic job.

Now to the very dear friend who proof read this book after the editing and all the changes had been made. Roger Feehan. Thank you Roger for your help and expertise. Your patience with me was invaluable. You gave Eileen a much needed rest from her labours after the mammoth task of proof reading my first two books.

And the last thank you goes to my precious, very clever, handsome boy for producing the final layout for the book, the PDF file and, of course, for the fabulous cover. It looks amazing and goes wonderfully alongside my first two books. You have done your mother proud once again.

I am very blessed, and so grateful for all the help, patience and love I have been given from ALL my family and friends.

If I have forgotten anyone please forgive me.

One last thing, I would be amiss if I didn't finally thank that wonderful man I call 'husband' for his patience. I only burnt his tea once in the writing of this book, but he found me with tears streaming down my face on more than one occasion.

Blessings to each and every one of you.

FOREWORD

By Jean Charlton

The Angels Bade you pick up your pen
To receive and write with love these poems within

To young and old - messages and greetings
Of hopeful peace and celestial meetings.

These beautiful poems received and written with dedication faith and love, span decades of the writer's wonderful and personal journey. Dip into their depth and you will endeavour to find a prose to calm and warm your spirit.

My friendship with Isabella started thirty years ago when we moved to a house in the same street. We met through our children who played together enjoying the carefree life of the young.
Isabella and I soon became close friends and met and talked together on many subjects.
I remember the sad day her Father passed, and the grief within her family.
I started to go and visit her in the quiet of the evening when our children were all asleep, and we spoke of life without those we loved. One evening on my visit she told me with amazement that she had heard her Father's voice. Isabella was so happy, it soothed her grieving Spirit. She then showed me a poem he had written through her. As you can imagine I was amazed. Could this possibly be true? But indeed it was, and many wonderful poems were to follow.
Isabella was now able to hear voices, but what she really longed for was to be able to see. That of course came later.
What a wonderful gift this was to receive these extraordinary poems from her Father and eventually to see his dear face.
This was the beginning of an incredible journey.

Next came the power from her hands, the power of helping to calm and heal those in distress.

I myself had healing from those very hands, together with my son who had such faith in Aunty Issy that I had to bring her to my home very late one evening. He severely burnt his hand while playing with petrol. I witnessed for myself her healing and calming influence on my distressed child.

There are many people today who can vouch for the help and peace she has given them.

We came into each other's lives at the right time. I was always willing to be there to listen to Isabella as she moved forward on this journey, helping each and every soul who came to receive this wonderful gift of healing.

God bless you Isabella.

INTRODUCTION

I'm sure as you picked this book of poems off the shelf you would probably have been asking yourself, who is this woman and what possessed her to write this book? And those are both valid questions.

So here are the answers.

I am a wife, mother and grandmother and, as I mentioned in my second book, I love my life. I have been married to my husband for forty-five years and we are just starting to have some fun. May God grant us both many more years together.

I have been blessed to be able to still hear our loved ones' voices after they leave us here on earth. In other words I am clairaudient and because of this I have been writing spirit messages and poems from our loved ones since 1983. I guess in anyone's book that's quite a long time. Subsequently I have many - and I do mean many! messages and poems to share with you. That is me in a nutshell. And these messages are what this book is all about.

It's all the beautiful, wonderful words that have come from Heaven for me to share with you.

I make no apologies for the fact most of the poems / stories that you will read in the coming pages are a bit religious in their tone. I was brought up in a very religious household. My father was a Methodist lay preacher and most of the poems were written by him. But you'll be pleased to know he did have a good sense of humour and this shines through in some of his writing. Obviously my upbringing has left a mark on me. I will however apologise if I offend anyone in anyway by any of the words that are written down. So if your religious beliefs are different from mine and my father's, I do hope you can read the following poems and stories with a loving heart and put your own interpretations/slant on each and every one of them. I wouldn't call myself religious, but I would call myself Spiritual.

Let's just all enjoy the wonderful kind and caring words that have been sent from another realm.

They were all miracles to me at the time I wrote each of them down and they are still miracles to me, to this day.

Talking of miracles, perhaps the miracle of me writing began much further back in my life than I ever realised. I'm saying that because I've just taken a step back into my own childhood. I have an amazingly clear picture of me in my school uniform when I was about fourteen years old (I look so young and naive). I did mention to you in book two how I love it when I'm with a patient and I suddenly find myself looking into one of their past lives. Well guess what, I've just stepped back over fifty years into this life of mine.

CHAPTER ONE

MY MEMORY FILE

If you had asked me when I was fourteen years old if I would ever write a book and have it published, I might have hesitated for a few minutes, but then I think I would have answered you and said "yes".

And here's the reason why.

Our Headmaster at school at the time had decided in his wisdom to hold a speech competition. This had never been done in the history of our school and the criteria for entry was to be by virtue of a 'writing competition'.

Thinking back, this was very clever of him. He had the whole school animated and buzzing with excitement for weeks before the event, not least because a television personality was going to be invited to our school to judge the competition. This was major and I mean major for both pupils and teachers alike.

It was 1964 and a lot of families with children in our school didn't own their own television set. Televisions were a luxury item and we also need to remember that those families that were lucky enough to have one watched everything in black and white. Colour TV's had not been invented (I know, the Dark Ages) let alone the chance to see a TV personality up close and in the flesh.

A panel of our teachers were chosen to judge the essay competition and the date and time for all the essays to be written was chosen by the Head. This day affectionately became known as D Day. In assembly, on the morning of D Day, every pupil in our school was handed a list of six titles to choose from for the competition. We were all told to look over the list and try and choose the title we thought we could write about with the most enthusiasm. I can still remember chuckling quietly to myself when I chose mine.

There were two classes in each school year and whoever came top of their class with their essay would then go forward to the speech competition and read their essays out loud to the whole school. This was even going to include all the non-teaching staff and of course the TV celebrity who, together with the help of four of our teachers, would choose the top three pupils. Our celebrity guest would then choose the overall winner.

This was all so exciting. From our teachers to the dinner ladies to the cleaning staff and even the school caretaker, everyone in the school was looking forward to 'speech day'. The whole thing was treated like a military operation. Every class in the school sat down at two o'clock on the chosen day. Each form teacher was told we had one and a half hours to write our essays. Our essay books were handed out and we all began.

I loved my fountain pen full of turquoise ink, yes turquoise. It was my favourite colour at the time. No black or blue ink for me. I can still see myself sitting at my desk in the classroom in the front row, right in front of the teacher's desk and every fifteen minutes or so Mr Gilmore (our English teacher and form master) had a stroll around our classroom. Every time he walked past my desk he stopped and looked over my shoulder, obviously reading what I had written so far. And each and every time he chuckled quietly to himself. He was obviously enjoying reading what I had just written, nearly as much as I was enjoying writing it.

When I had read slowly down the list of titles we were given to choose from that morning one had stood out on the page from the rest as if it had been written in bright red ink and that title was 'The lesson which I think is a waste of time'. When I read the words I started chuckling to myself and I knew in an instant exactly what I wanted to write. My 'waste of time lesson' had always been History. So as soon as my brain had registered my choice, my mind started working overtime. In fact, I began to worry in case I wouldn't have enough time to complete my task.

I could never understand why I had to learn about some of the uninteresting events that happened in the past. I always wanted to learn about the future and I had spent the previous four and a half years asking my history teacher the exact same question, so this title was perfect for me. I wanted to learn about space travel (please remember Neil Armstrong didn't set foot on the moon for another five years). I wanted to learn about life on other planets. Was there a way I could travel backwards through time so that I could go and witness events that I myself was interested in? Not the boring things I was forced to study. Was there a way to travel into the future? Were there any doorways in space that we could travel through from our planet? Trust me, I had asked some of my teachers the very same questions. So my essay was no surprise to a few of them (strange child, that was my label, and it's no wonder when I think back).

Pens down.

Well, I'd written it and I managed to get everything down on paper that I wanted to.

I knew I'd written a good essay, I just knew. The words just seemed to flow from my pen without me even trying.

But was it good enough to win? Only time would tell.

We all handed in our essay books to our teachers, packed our bags and left our classrooms because it was now home time.

Two weeks later, during an English lesson, into our classroom walked, or should I say marched, the Headmaster and before Mr Gilmore had a chance to say anything the Head said, as he shook my essay book in front of Mr Gilmore's face, "did she write this herself? Did she do this herself?" He gave Mr Gilmore the chance to look at what he was 'shaking' and then Mr Gilmore answered him: "Yes, she wrote it herself. I watched her as every word was scribed onto the page. There is no argument or skulduggery going on here. I can categorically say Isabella wrote this essay all by herself."

"Then, in that case, she has just won the writing competition for this class," and, with that, he turned and walked out of the door with a quick grin in my direction.

Wow.

I'd won.

"I knew you would win; that was an excellent essay. Well done."

"Thank you Mr Gilmore."

At Speech Day four weeks later I walked out onto the stage in our assembly hall to a sea of expectant faces (the whole school had heard I had written something about space travel and they couldn't wait to hear it). The hall was packed out. You could have heard a pin drop, it was so quiet. And there below me in the front row, right in front of the lectern I was to spread my essay out onto was our Headmaster. (He always made me nervous.) As my eyes followed the centre aisle to the back of the hall I spotted our honoured guest sitting on a very large chair. I can even remember thinking to myself at the time. "Where did they get that from?" (the chair) and, "Oh gosh, he does look orange again."

I've forgotten to tell you this.

Our honoured guest had called into our school the previous week to finalise his schedule and meet the Headmaster and, as you can imagine, all the pupils (including me) were hanging out of windows, peering round doors, cramming corridors and lining the drive as he drove his car to the front door (a bit of an exaggeration but you get the picture), all of us desperately trying to catch a glimpse of him. Yes, it was a 'him' and I can tell you now we were all in fits of giggles when we did catch sight of him because his skin was a very strange-looking shade of orange and he had very unnaturally bright red lips. His make-up artist in 1964 had not done a very good job of his fake tan or make-up and we all thought he looked hilarious.

The school lectern was directly in front of me.

In the absolute silence of our assembly hall, I took my time as I spread out my essay onto the lectern just in case I needed to refer to it. (I had learnt it by heart but all the contestants were told to make sure we had our essays to read in case our nerves got the better of us.) Then I took hold of, or should I say I clung onto, the sides of the lectern to stop myself from wobbling because I could feel my knees knocking. I stood as still as I could, took a deep breath and recited my essay in a very clear, decisive voice, secretly enjoying every minute of my fame. The school hall erupted into applause when I finished and our Headmaster couldn't contain himself. He stood up and when the clapping subsided he turned and said to the audience, "I think, without doubt, everyone in this hall today would love the answers to some of the questions Isabella has just asked. Well done, young lady," and, with that, he sat down to his own round of applause.

Did I win? I'm sure you can guess the answer.

The first announcement was to say who the top three contestants were; my name was the last to be read out. I can still remember standing on the stage with all the other contestants, shaking like a leaf, and then our celebrity guest stood up to announce the overall winner and said my name; that's when I burst into tears.

But they were happy tears.

I knew I was meant to win the whole competition from the moment I put my pen to paper on the day I entered the writing competition. I had the best of days writing my winning essay. My sixth sense had been working overtime for me that day and my 'voice', the voice that has been with me since I was a child, told me I would win. So I think when the invited celebrity read my name out as the winner and the whole school erupted into applause especially for me I was overcome with happy emotions.

There were some very good essays, there were some very good speakers, but because my essay was so different from the others it had stood out and I narrated it well because I *felt* every word that I'd written.

I have never forgotten that day. I was a star for the day. I was a celebrity not just for that day but for a few days and weeks afterwards and, I've got to be honest with you, I loved every minute of it.

But what I remember most about the whole event, with the biggest smile, was the day I sat at my desk with my pen full of turquoise ink as I wrote my essay.

If you've never written anything of any note yourself, you may not be able to understand what I'm about to say but if, on the other hand, you have then you will know exactly what I mean. When you are in full flow, writing away as if each word has been placed into your head especially for you to use just in the right place, it's like magic. I loved the way my thoughts just flowed that day, filling my mind with the words I needed to put onto the page in front of me and that's what it was like for me when I wrote my first two books. And I hope that's what's going to happen for me again now.

I love writing, I love telling stories and I've waited many years to write this particular book. Why? Because I made myself (and my father) a promise many years ago - that one day I would write all of my father's poems and messages and those from other people down in a book. This is that book. At least it's the start. Because I think I have far too many poems for just one book.

What I'm hoping will make this compilation a little bit different from other books in the same genre is that I'm not only going to share with you many of the poems my father and other souls have given me, I am also going to tell you the stories behind each of them, if there is a story to tell. Because the stories were also part of the learning experiences I was to have.

None of the words in the poems and messages that I'm going to write down in the following pages are mine. I wish they were I really do. I would love to be able to say to you all, "look how clever I am." But, I can't, and I promise you I haven't stolen them. They were recited/given to me with much love, to help us all understand that this life is only a small part of a far greater picture and plan than any of us could ever imagine.

Many of the poems that I have scribed are for us all to read and enjoy, some of them were especially written for individuals for very special reasons. It is with these poems that I would like to begin this book.

I do hope you enjoy reading them and perhaps you will also be able to take something away from them for yourself.

I will write the stories first so that you can get a clear picture as to the reasons why each of the poems or messages were written and then, I will follow with the words sent from the Spirit world.

The first poems I ever wrote were way back in 1983 and the following story is the reason why they were written - so here goes...

CHAPTER TWO

MARY'S STORY

As my father and mother were leaving the little chapel they attended on a cold frosty November night in 1983, my father offered to drive the minister home. The minister gratefully accepted. Dad explained to him that he and my mother had walked the short distance from home to the chapel, so they all needed to walk back to their home to get the car.

Following them out of the chapel were two elderly sisters, Mary and Eve. They were always the last to leave because they held the keys to the chapel and they always locked up. Eve had heard the conversation my father had with the minister and invited my mother home with her and Mary for supper while dad drove the minister home but my mother declined. She told Eve that she would enjoy the walk home because it was such a lovely crisp, clear, starry night. My father then helped my mother and the minister across the main road because the road was very slippery, and then he watched as Eve walked very gingerly across the road to the pavement. My father turned around and joined my mother and the minister and they started to walk the short distance back home for Dad to get the car.

Within seconds of them all turning their backs my father told me he heard a screech of brakes followed by a very loud thud. Dad said his instincts took over and he turned around. At that point he said he had no idea as to exactly what had happened. All he could see was a car had crashed into the little stone wall that stood directly in front of the chapel. He ran across the road to see if he could help the people inside the car. He told me he breathed a sigh of relief when he saw that all the occupants were unhurt, thank God. The driver of the car then told my father that he had seen an old lady crossing the road and he had braked not realising he was on black ice. His car had then skidded across the road out of control and mounted the pavement and hit the wall. Dad told me he then looked around trying to take in the whole scene in front of him and that's when he spotted Eve looking very dazed and distressed.

It was then that he realised Mary was missing.

He told me that within a split second of him realising that Mary was nowhere to be seen, he will never forget the icy chill that crept over him, making him feel very uneasy. Without knowing what or why he was doing it he went to the front of the damaged car. He said he found it very difficult to see in the darkness. The only light shining was the light coming from the head lights. They were shining on the wall and that made it difficult to be able to see beneath the brightness of the beams.

When my father relayed this story to me, he told me that the blackness beneath the front of the car's lights felt very foreboding to him and that made him hesitate for a few seconds before he knelt down to look.

I know what he saw remained with him until his dying day.

He knelt down on the ground and that's when he found Mary lying like a rag doll. He told me he could hardly see her face and head because of all the blood. It was obvious to him that Mary was dead because her head was so severely damaged. Dad told me at that very instant he had the most horrible feeling that the devil himself was laughing at him as he stooped over Mary's shattered body.

It must have seemed to him as if he had just stepped into a scene from a horror movie, but it wasn't a movie, it was real.

Apparently my father's instant reaction was one of extreme anger.

He told me that he actually thumped down hard on the bonnet of the car three or four times. Please don't misunderstand, he wasn't angry with the people in the car, his anger was because of the horrible way in which Mary had died.

There were other people around who had witnessed the crash but because my father and his little party had had their backs turned away at the precise moment the accident occurred, they only found out later what the full events had been.

And this apparently is what happened.

When Eve had reached the pavement opposite the chapel she realised Mary was not behind her, so she started to re-cross the road to get her. She saw Mary coming out of the Chapel and watched as her bible slipped from her hand onto the ground, right beside the wall next to the chapel door. She then watched as Mary bent down to pick her bible up. At the exact same moment the driver of the car coming down the hill saw Eve re-crossing the road. He braked but skidded on the black ice, right across to the other side of the road where he mounted the pavement and hit Mary just as she was bending down. Dear Lord - that was why her head was so badly damaged and not her legs. The driver of the car said that he didn't even know that Mary was there. He never saw her. The whole episode was over in a matter of seconds.

My Mum best described Mary. She said she was so like the Mary described in the bible, full of God's love. I had the privilege of meeting her a few times over the previous years. She had spoken with a very gentle, quiet voice that seemed to embrace the person she was speaking to with love. She also had the most wonderful clear, bright blue, sparkling eyes. It was as if God himself was shining his love out into the world from inside of her.

Mary's death was to affect the village greatly.

For thirty years, Mary and Eve had kept the little chapel in the village open. When my mother and father moved into the area my father helped them. But after Dad died, and then Mary, the little chapel had to close after being open for over a hundred years. There is still sadness in the village apparently to this day because that little chapel is no more.

Mary and Eve had never married and they had lived together all of their lives. This made Mary's passing all the greater for Eve to bear.

18

About two weeks after the accident happened, I was sitting one evening going over in my mind the story my father had told me when a thought came to me. Perhaps I could try and write a poem for Eve in the hope it might give her some comfort, and for my parents because it was obvious they were also both grieving. I can't really recall very much about writing the two poems. At the time of writing I was very pleased with myself, because I honestly thought that 'I' had written them (stupid me). I do however clearly remember the day I took them to my parents so they could read them and then pass them on to Eve.

I can still see my father as if it was yesterday.

Dad and I were standing side by side looking out of the kitchen window into his beautiful garden. After my father had read and reread them both he must have asked me at least half a dozen times if "I" had written them? Was I absolutely sure I had written them? "Well, of course I wrote them Daddy, no one else was in the room with me at the time."

When my father gave them to Eve she apparently sat and read them a few times and cried. She told my father that she loved both of them and would he please tell me that she would treasure them both. Treasure the words I had written for her for the rest of her life.

For MARY

She was suddenly taken
we do not know why
by the Angels in Heaven
to live by His side

No rhyme or no reason
for this can we see
but we know that for certain
in Heaven she'll be

A more wonderful woman
on earth could you meet
our world will be sadder
in Heaven - more sweet

It is hard Lord to reason
why things should be so
but we'll understand, one day
of this I am sure

Give us the strength Lord
to stand tall today
knowing for certain
your love will prevail.

For Mary

May she rest in the arms of Jesus
may she smile when she sees His sweet face
may she join with the Angels in Praises
at His side, on her knees, by His feet

May she always be there in His presence
for her love for Him always shone through
she was everything He could have hoped for
she saw Him in all that we do

May the Lord take our sister dear Mary
may He tenderly keep her we pray
till the day that we join her in Heaven
help us Lord, bear our grief, till that day.

I'm sure both those two dear sisters are together now in their home far from earth. I would like to send them both my love and a hug and say it was a privilege to have known them.

CHAPTER THREE

FOR DARREL

This next story is very precious to me. I am going to tell it almost exactly as I wrote it the first time around. If I were to try and write it all again from scratch a second time, I know I will spoil the story telling because I will never be able to experience the same emotions I felt inside of me the first time I sat quietly recalling what happened so many years earlier.

A few months before our son's eighth birthday, at the same time he started a new school and without going into great detail, I will just say that in the small class of seven year old boys was a little boy called Darrel. Alexander didn't meet him until nearly the end of his first term because he was in hospital receiving treatment. When Darrel did return to school it was for a few hours only each day as he was very weak.

He had no hair when he came back to school due to the treatment he was receiving, but Alexander and the other boys in their class just didn't seem to notice. He was just another of their little pals. The only time Alexander talked about Darrel was the day he came home from school and told me that Darrel had been punched in his stomach by another boy and Alexander proudly announced that he had thumped the offender. This to the best of my knowledge, is the only time in our son's school years that he resorted to any sort of violence.

At a parents evening towards the end of the spring term, my son's teacher told me she had given them all an essay to write entitled 'my greatest wish'. Please remember the boys were only seven years old. Nearly every little boy in the class had written that they wished that Darrel would get well. She told me she cried her way through marking their work and I stood and cried as she told me.

I never actually met Darrel personally, but I often saw him when I and the other parents picked up their children from the school gate at home time. He was always picked up by his grandmother who was looking after him. It was much later that I found out that he lived with his grandparents most of the time.

As that year progressed, his condition deteriorated and he was unable to attend school during most of the summer term. The boys kept in touch by writing to him and sending him pictures every week letting him know what was going on in their class. When the children broke up for the summer holidays, Darrel was dangerously ill.

Tea time on Friday the third of August 1984, as I was making our evening meal, our telephone rang. It was a friend of mine who also had a son in the same year as Darrel and she was crying. She told me that she had just heard that he had died and the funeral was to be on the following Tuesday. Then she asked me if I would be going. I said no, as I didn't know the family and I didn't want to intrude because I was very aware the church would be packed to the rafters. I put the phone down and burst into tears.

This was all so close.

A child the same sex, the same age and more importantly a friend of our son had died. I managed to finish making the family meal between my tears by which time Alexander found me crying. After telling him as gently as I could that Darrel had gone to heaven, I was amazed by his response. "He'll be safe now mummy and he won't be in anymore pain, his tummy hurt, but it won't now." From the mouths of babes, he actually made me feel better. He did have a few tears but looking back I'm sure he was upset because I was upset.

It was normal for me to be up late at night as I had paperwork to do and the best time for me to do it was when everyone had gone to bed and the house was very quiet - this night was no exception.

I sat down beside the fire with the coffee table in front

24

of me all ready to do my work, but I couldn't get Darrel out of my mind. As the night wore on I became more upset. I remember thinking to myself that I was being totally irrational, I didn't even know him but that didn't help and it didn't stop me from crying.

Words kept going through my mind.

A little soul went home today. The words kept repeating themselves over and over and over again. What made me write them down I honestly couldn't say but I did and as I kept looking at them a thought came into my mind. Perhaps I could write some words of comfort for Darrel's family, as I had done for Mary's sister the previous year. But the harder I tried to write the more confused I became.

By this time it was about three thirty in the morning and even by my late hours this was way past my bed time. But something was keeping me up. I was absolutely exhausted. I had cried more in the last few hours than I had in years yet there was no real logical explanation. My mind was now completely worn out, almost blank. That's when the words started to flow. It was as if I were plugged into a dictating machine.

Each and every time the 'I' in me had tried to write, the words just wouldn't come. But once I stopped trying to write myself, the words flowed with ease. I soon realised that the words were being given to me from somewhere in the Spiritual realm, but from where exactly, I wasn't sure.

It was about six o'clock in the morning when the poem was finished. I was physically and emotionally exhausted. I read through the words many times, they were so simple and beautiful. The poem was not for me, but clearly for Darrel's family. But what could I do? Should I try and get it to them? Was I being presumptuous in thinking I should even try? What a night.

I knew if I gave myself anytime to think, the logical side of my nature would take over and the poem would end up in the bottom of a drawer in our home, never to be seen or read again. So at nine o'clock in the morning (I never did get to bed)

I rang our son's school. Even though it was the summer holidays and Saturday, there was a good chance the headmaster would be in his study as he lived on the premises. It was the only way I knew of to get Darrel's family's address. My luck was in, or as I'm now sure was the case, the powers that be made sure he was there for me. The headmaster answered the telephone. I didn't want to go into the real reason for wanting the address, so I told him that we had just heard about Darrel dying, and we wanted to send a card to the family from Alexander. He was more than happy to oblige, as he knew that Alexander had been a friend.

Having checked my A/Z of the area to find the street where the family lived, I got into my car. I must have looked like last week's dinner, I could hardly see out of my eyes they were so puffed up, but I was determined to deliver the poem, before I gave myself a chance to change my mind.

You can't begin to imagine how I felt, what right had I to presume the family would be interested in the poem, they might be very annoyed and angry with me. They might think me a total crank. All these thoughts and many more were pouring through my mind as I drove to their home. It didn't take me long to find the street and the house, but I was so nervous I parked the car on the opposite side of the road, and sat shaking for ages before I gathered up the courage to walk up the path to their front door.

Having knocked on the door, I was about to leave when an older gentleman answered it. All I could say was. 'I'm so sorry' as I handed him the envelope in which I had placed the poem. I turned around and walked away.

Well, I'd done it now, at least (I thought) they don't know me, so if they are angry they wouldn't be able to find me, what a muddled mess I was in.

Having spent what I can only describe as a lost weekend, I decided to have a few days off work. I was shattered. Monday came and went, but on Tuesday while I was sitting having a cup of tea late in the afternoon, the telephone rang, my friend again. She had been to Darrel's funeral. The telling was as I expected, the church had been packed out with family, friends, parents, teachers and the headmaster, who apparently stood with tears streaming down his face along with everyone else during the service. But the next thing she told me made my heart miss a beat.

After the opening hymn, the Vicar had stood up and then picked up an envelope, explaining to the congregation that a lady had hand delivered it to the family. He said he was going to read the poem instead of the usual funeral service as the family felt it said everything they wanted to say - that there was no need for any other words.

My reaction, firstly great relief (at least they weren't annoyed with me) and then, I think, pleased. At first with myself, but after a few seconds thought and remembering that I knew I hadn't written the words, just pleased I had been able to hear the words, and secondly the courage to follow my instincts and deliver it to the family.

That summer was a time I'm never going to forget.

The rest of the year came and went without any more unusual experiences for me and, in fact, so did most of the following year and for that I was thankful, but the story doesn't end there.

The following Christmas, seventeen months after Darrel passed over, my husband and I attended our sons school Christmas dinner dance. During the evening one of the other mums said to me "Did you know Darrel's grandparents are here this evening and did you know that he lived with them most of the time?" I answered "no, on both counts." She pointed Darrel's grandmother out to me.

What made me go over to her I really can't say but she did look very approachable and cosy. I apologised for bothering her and then I said, "I know you don't know me, but I'm the lady who handed..."

She didn't give me the chance to finish my sentence. She took hold of both my arms just below my elbows as tears started to gently fall down her face.

"You'll never know, you'll just never know what that poem meant to us all."

She let go of my arms opened her handbag and pulled out what was by now a very crumpled-looking envelope.

"I carry this with me always. I read it every morning and every night, it's the one thing that has helped to keep me going."

By this time the tears were streaming down my face. She tried to thank me but I stopped her and tried to explain to her that the words were not mine, they had been given to me because her need had been so great. After a lovely cuddle I wished her well and left her side. I wasn't much good for the rest of the dance but I had the most wonderful warm feeling deep down inside me. For once in my life I had done something very worthwhile. Not just the writing of the poem but following my intuition in taking the poem to the family when the logical side of me had desperately not wanted to.

Over the next few years, I was to visit the family with messages from Darrel for his grandparents and his mother. It was the most wonderful comfort for them all.

The only reason I have been able to scribe this with so much accuracy is because I wrote this all down in long hand at the time. I took it to Darrel's grandparents in 1991 to let them read through it all and asked them, if in the years to come, I was ever to write a book would they like me to include Darrel's story. They both said they would. I was to write the story with their blessings. I promised I would. I have now kept that promise.

3rd August 1984 for Darrel's Family

A little Soul went home today
to peace and rest and love
his Heavenly father welcomed him
to his Heavenly home above

The pain he felt confusion too
have all now gone away
and we are left to mourn our loss
on this, our saddest day

Lord, please be with his family
let them lean upon your arm
and help them through the coming days
with peace and love and calm

Be with them Lord and let them know
that you have got him safe
until the day, when one by one
they shall see his smiling face.

Oh boy, where are the hankies?

It gets me every time.

I guess it's not going to matter how many years pass by, Darrel's story and his poem are going to get to me each and every time I recall and read them. Tears are going to come into my eyes and stream down my face without fail as the memories from that time in my life all come flooding back.

I hope you enjoyed reading it as much as I did.

Now I would like to share with you the words that Darrel himself sent to his grandparents about four years after he passed over, and I'm also going to tell you about the time Darrel's mum came to see me.

About eight days before Christmas, just after I had written a lovely Christmas poem from my father, I had a most unexpected visitor. I heard a young boy's voice in my ear and I instinctively knew who the voice belonged to - Darrel.

I had never actually heard his voice before that night, but he was very clear and very excited to be talking to me. He told me he had come to me, to ask me to take a message to his Grandparents. He said they had been very down during the past year. They apparently were still missing him and were worried in case he was not alright.

He then told me he had tried to let them know that he was okay, but they didn't seem to be aware of him, however but his little brother was. Apparently, he was also living with his grandparents, just as Darrel had done. His brother had only been one year old when Darrel had passed over. He said he often went to talk to him. He then told me that his brother could both see and hear him. Would I please write the message down and take it to them. I said of course I would.

The words he gave me to write were very funny. I had almost forgotten he was just twelve years old. I finished writing his words down for him, he thanked me, and then he disappeared. Typical, just like my own son, they get what they want, say thanks, and are gone.

Even though it had been four years since I delivered the poem that I'd written for Darrel's family, I could still remember where they lived. Their house was only two streets away from where Nansi (my old friend and healer) now lived. So, after tea the following day, I once again found myself knocking on their front door, but this time I didn't make a quick exit when Darrel's grandfather answered it.

I explained why I had come and he immediately invited me into the house and into their lounge. Grandma came into the room from their kitchen and gave me a big hug, recognising me immediately.

While I sat and explained to them that Darrel had come to me the previous night - and given me a message for them all - I had not known that his little brother was in the next room, listening to me from behind the door. Halfway through me reading them Darrel's message his little brother ran into the room shouting. "That's from my brother, that's my brother." I said, "yes, your brother gave me the words last night."

"He comes to talk to me when I'm in my bedroom."

I said, "That's wonderful for you. He's around you all a lot."

"I know he is."

I asked his grandparents, "What does he mean about making you jump?"

His grandfather said, "We often know when he's about because he makes cups, dinner plates and all sorts of things move across the kitchen bench. We were worried in case he was upset about something. We kept asking ourselves, is he alright?

"I think you've got your answer. He was concerned enough to come to me and give me the message for you, because he knew you were worried. I just think this is so lovely."

His grandparents both sat down beside me and cried with joy. They said it was the best Christmas present they could ever have wished for. After lots of hugs from them all, I left.

For me writing the words from Darrel and delivering it to his family had been a small thing. But for his family, it had meant the world and yes, it gave me a lovely warm feeling inside.

And here are the words that Darrel gave me that night.

For Darrel's Grandparents from Darrel

I'm so happy now it's Christmas
I can see the fairy lights
Christmas trees and all the sparkles
brightening up the darkest night

In our world of sunshine
where the sun is bright all day
we have no need of bright things
all our life is bright and gay

We are always happy
nothing can or does harm us
we are well and full of laughter
no one's naughty or gets cross

Please Gran I can come and see you
any time I choose to go
from my place of shining beauty
to you earth so far below

Sometimes I come and watch you
especially at the kitchen sink
cooking things and washing dishes
I sometimes try and make things slip

I am happy and so well looked after
in my home now way up high
I'm strong and growing quickly
you'd be just so proud I'm tall and strong

When Christmas comes and you're all sad
because I'm not with you
I am — it's just you can't see me
but I can see all of you.

Another year went by and just as Christmas was fast approaching, who should come to call again, Darrel. This time he wasn't worried about his family he just wanted me to take a Christmas message to his family. And these are the words he gave me on the 13th December 1989 for his grandparents, his brother and his mother.

The Christmas Tree

I've watched you all this year you know
I've worked and played with you
I know I've been a pest at times
because I've bothered you

I know I shouldn't really try
to make you jump — oh heck
but Grandad loves to know its me
the Christmas tree's a wreck
(well — not quite)

I love to see the fairy lights
they sparkle and they glow
I'll go and visit Edison
he'll teach me all he knows

My teachers help me learn so fast
my school's a special place
it doesn't matter how I do
because there is no race

Christmas means so much to you
the trees and all the toys
the presents that Gran wraps with care
to bring each one some joy

You really should be happy Gran
I shine just like your tree
you're both my special people
please keep shining just for me.

Taken, delivered and received, with lots of love and cuddles.

Darrel's grandparents knew where I lived, and in actual fact at the time I only lived about two miles from them. So when I received a phone call in 1991 from Darrel's mum, who I had never met, I was not surprised. She rang me to ask if she could come and see me, she said she desperately wanted to see me to talk to me about Darrel. So on a cold winter's evening in 1991, some seven years after Darrel had left us here on earth, she came to my home for a visit.

She was so nervous. I can only hope I was able to make her feel comfortable and welcome, warm fire, mug of coffee, and a big hug all within minutes of her entering our home.

As she sat herself down on our settee a young man entered the room and sat himself down on the arm of the chair right next to his mother. Yes, Darrel had also come to join us.

Perfect timing.

Of course our sons were now fourteen years old. My own son was over six feet tall at this point, and Darrel was not much shorter. He was a very tall, fair-haired handsome young man, who any mother would have been proud to call son.

His mother immediately asked me if Darrel was with us in the room and I said, "yes."

She said, "I thought he was, I can feel him."

Darrel was able to communicate with his mother through me. But I've got to be honest here and say I can still picture him sitting on the arm of our settee all those years ago but I can't remember what he said to his mother. But I'm sure she does, because of course everything he was saying was for her, not me. About a month after she had been for her visit, I received a lovely letter from her thanking me for the visit and all the things she heard from Darrel. I've still got the letter. But before she left me that evening I gave her a file with some of my father's poems. My hope was that they would help her in some small way. I'm going to quote a couple of lines from the letter that she sent me on the 25th November 1991, to let you know the part my father's poems played in helping her.

"The book of poems are a great comfort. I often take them out when I'm all alone and read through different ones trying to get a glimpse or to try and understand the place in which Darrel is in now. To understand brings me closer if you understand what I mean."

But that's not the end of this story.

One evening in February 1992, the 19th to be exact, just after I had scribed some more of my father's words, I heard a voice and I recognised it immediately, Darrel.

He explained to me that he was very worried about his grandparents and his mum and he wanted to get a message to them all. So here are the words that he gave me that night.

Hi

They're both not very well you know
but my brothers doing fine
he knows I'm still around him
and I will be for all time

Please give them both some kisses
for they're feeling very low
and they need to know I'm with them
I spend most of my time below

I do still do my lessons
and I've learned much for my years
I'm feeling very sorry for my old pals
especially this year

Please give Mam a big hug
she still knows I'm very near
and tell her that I see her
when she has her quiet tears

It's very hard for me sometimes
when I see them all upset
the pain for them has eased some
but the past they won't forget

They still think of me as suffering
they remember how I felt
tell them that's all over
it went the day the real me left

I can't even remember
so please tell them to let go
I left the pain behind me
it's time they all let go

Lots and lots of love to all
I'm sending them my best
it's great to get this message through
that's got it off my chest

I've waited for the right time
the time you need it most
it wouldn't mean so much to you
if I popped up like a ghost
(well it rhymes)

I've read the story that's been wrote
I'm finally going in print
I think that I'll be famous
boy what will my pals all think
fame at last.

Darrel now fifteen years old.

After my first book was published in 2014 I somehow managed to find Darrel's grandparents' address and as the powers that be would have it, they still lived in the very same house that I had visited thirty years earlier when I delivered that very first poem to them, just after Darrel died in August 1984.

I was able to arrange to visit them.

My intentions were to give Darrel's grandparents a copy of the book as a present so that they would have a record of Darrel's story. The story they gave me permission to put into print nearly thirty years earlier.

Just as I was leaving our home with their copy of the book safely on the front seat of my car beside me, something made me go back into the house and get a second copy of my book to take with me.

When I got to the house and rang the doorbell, who should answer the door but Darrel's mum who I had not seen or heard from since 1991. She invited me into the house at which point Darrel's grandfather came to welcome me with a big hug. The sadness for me was that grandma had died the previous year so she was not there to greet me (not in flesh anyway), but she was most definitely in the room with us that afternoon.

I sat and read them both the stories from the book and I've got to be honest with you, I was reading it through my tears. Even though thirty years had gone by it is still a very emotional story if you are connected to it in any way and, of course, I was and still am. Both his grandfather and his mother were overjoyed to hear it and to each be given a copy.

After a cup of tea and a lovely chat with them both, I left with a very warm feeling in my tummy and it wasn't the hot drink.

I had kept my promise and they both had a gift they would treasure.

CHAPTER FOUR

BOOK DEDICATION

Chapter four might seem a very strange place to be putting my book dedication page, but actually this is the perfect place and as you read on, you will understand why it's not at the front of the book.

Written below are the exact words I wrote down in 1988 a few weeks after my father dictated his first amazing messages to me.

Little did I know at the time he would be so prolific when I filed them into a lovely two ringed silver binder. That binder is now overflowing and right at the front I typed and placed the following words, my dedication. So here they are just as the front page appears in what is now a very scruffy looking binder with over one hundred poems inside all full of love and wonder. All sent from the great beyond.

DEDICATION

I dedicate the pages that follow to three very precious Souls.

Firstly to my dear father who passed this life on the 9th March 1988, without his love to me these words could never have been written down. Love builds bridges and the greatest bridge of all is between our world and the next. I hear his voice so clearly and I have dictated his wonderful words as clearly and precisely as my human ear can hear. I pray that he forgives me if anything has been wrongly scribed.

Secondly, I dedicate with my love these pages to my mother. Without her this wonderful gift may never have been used.

And last but not least to the most wonderful husband whose patience and understanding has sustained me in more ways than I can ever tell, and he will ever know.

To these three dear Souls we owe this book.

A few days after my father passed this life in March 1988 my mother said to me, "Wouldn't it be wonderful if I could get a letter from your father?"

I can't remember the exact conversation we were having at the time or why she said those words to me and in all the years that followed I never thought to ask her. But said them she did and that very night Mum got her letter.

Now, before I begin to write my father's words down I need to explain something to you all and to be able to do that I need to go back to when I lived at home with my parents. Finding the right words to use is always a bit of a worry for me. I just hope that I explain myself in such a way that you will understand, without a shadow of doubt, just how I felt the very first night that I heard my father's voice, after he passed into the world of Spirit.

So goes.

My memories in brief from my childhood and teenage years go something like this, because of what at the time I was not allowed.

No trousers, they were for boys not girls. Jeans for me were a complete no no.

Denim was the work of the devil.

No makeup, not even lipstick and most definitely no nail varnish and God forbid eye shadow.

The same handmade clothes as my sister (I've got to be honest and admit they were lovely) who was six years younger than me!

No showing of any flesh. No arms or neck or shoulders (or chest) on show and definitely no legs.

No bad language.

No drinking of alcohol.

No outward show of any affection.

No loud music.

No dancing or having fun.

No radio allowed and headphones did not exist in the 1950's.

No books.

No television past tea time.

And that was my life!!!

And any reference to being able to see or hear from a world beyond ours - The Devil's Work!!!

My next memory is probably the most important one to be telling you for the point that I'm trying to make.

As far as my father was concerned anyone who said they could see or speak to spirit people had to be mentally unstable because no one could see or speak to spirit people. He had told me on numerous occasions over the years that there was a gulf between our world and the next and that gulf could not be crossed. So anyone who said they could speak to departed Souls was telling lies and that's what my father and mother had believed all their lives. That's what my mother had been taught by her parents (they were great chapel people) and that's what my father had learnt from his religion. Mum had been brought up in a strict (but very loving) Methodist home and Dad had found his way into the Methodist faith, probably in his youth and possibly through my mother. She was just sixteen years old when they met and fell in love. I don't actually know how my father came to be a Methodist (his parents weren't great Chapel people that I know of). I never did ask him.

Anyway, Dad not only found God through the Methodist Chapel, he became a Methodist Lay Preacher man himself. Consequently, from being a young man my father had no time for anything to do with what he called spiritualism.

My father's word in our home was the law we all lived by and Dad never changed his mind once it was made up

So, there was no way on earth I could ever expect to hear my father's voice at any time after he passed into the Spirit world. Not one day after, or a thousand and one days after, let alone before we had buried him in the ground!

That's what made what happened next so **incredibly amazing for me.**

As a small child I heard spirit voices (and I saw Spirit people and more) but the only time I told my parents that I could hear people talking to me, they told me in no uncertain terms not to be so silly and of course there was that damn gulf they kept telling me about, so I never mentioned it to them again.

I kept quiet.

I hope I have succeeded in helping you understanding that never in a million trillion years did I ever expect to hear my father's voice ever again after he left this life.

Now I think I can get back to my story telling.

This is now the story that I wrote down in my first book almost as I wrote it.

On the third night after my father passed into the spirit world I was sitting on my own after my family had all gone to bed and I was crying. Let's be honest, I was very distressed. To say I was crying was an understatement and I was saying out loud to the air around me. "I'm going to miss you Daddy. I'm going to miss you so much. Are you anywhere near me? Can you hear me? Are you there Daddy." And I kept saying these words over and over in my distressed state.

And to my complete and utter amazement and that's got to be the understatement of the century I heard my father's voice answer me back.

There was no mistaking it.

His voice was as clear as day.

It was just as if he was standing right next to me having a normal conversation with me as if nothing had happened, just as if he was still very much alive.

44

He told me he had a message for my mother and would I please go and get a pad of paper and a pencil so that I could write his words down for him.

I did exactly as he asked as if I was on autopilot.

Even though this all happened many years ago the memory of that night is still so very clear.

I can still remember my exact thoughts.

'I must be going mad because this could not really be happening?' But Dad's voice is so clear. 'How could this be happening? Dad didn't believe in this sort of thing. I must be imagining this.' But something inside of me knew better than to doubt my own ears and hearing.

I followed my father's instructions to the letter as if someone had pressed the on button on a robot.

I somehow managed to find a pencil and a pad of paper through my swollen teary eyes and dripping nose and I sat myself down on our settee with the pad of paper on my lap even though I had absolutely no idea what was about to happen or what I was about to write.

I was shaking.

I was crying.

But I can clearly remember a feeling of excitement rising up inside of my stomach.

Let's face it, I was a bundle of mixed emotions and I will never have the correct words to use to be able to describe my exact feelings to you. But above everything, my heart was singing with pure happiness. My father was with me, speaking to me, and I knew beyond a shadow of doubt that I was actually hearing him. And then my father started to dictate his words to me.

What a state I was in, a complete jumble of indescribable human emotions.

My father had died just three nights ago but I could hear his voice, and I was sitting writing his words down.

I was going to miss him more than words could ever say, but he was here with me now. Even though I couldn't see him, I could hear him so very clearly. Could this be right or was I imagining it? Was I going crazy because of the grief I was experiencing??? Then he finished speaking and I finished writing.

And he was gone!

I just sat there and read and reread over and over again the words that Dad had given me. It was like a letter, or perhaps it was a poem, but it was most definitely for my mother. I just sat there that night in complete and utter shock and amazement and I cried - and I cried - and I cried.

And here are the words that he sent my mother on one of the most memorable nights of my life.

For You Dear

For all the love and all the tears
we shared together dear
our love goes on
it knows no bounds
believe me when I say
I'm with you ever by your side
I'm with you ever more

To give you joy and peace
believe in Him
that gave His life that we may all have peace
trust in our love
until the day I'll hold your hand

Your hear my voice
I call to you
yet you remain unsure
how can I make you understand
that love just has no bounds

I come across the great divide
time may seem long
but time apart
Gods grace will see you through
I'm walking just beyond your place
waiting just for you

My love to all I left behind
this pen will say it all
you must believe that what I say
is from me
your one and all.

God Bless

47

I could so easily skip over this and continue on with what happened the following morning but what had just happened to me was a once in a lifetime event; and for all the other amazing things that have happened to me over the years, that particular night almost tops the list. I'm writing this as tears are gently falling down my face, just remembering. It's thirty years since this all happened and that night is still crystal clear in my mind because it was so special.

As soon as I got up the following morning, I rang my mother. I was so excited I could hardly contain myself. I garbled to her that Dad had come to me last night and he had dictated a message for her. I kept saying to her that she has asked for a letter and Dad had sent you one. I must have read it to her at least three times. She sounded very bemused on the other end of the telephone. I promised her I would bring it with me to give to her in a few days time when I was due to visit her and I rang off.

About fifteen minutes later our telephone rang, it was my sister.

"Have you just rang Mum and read something to her." I told her I had. I explained what had happened and she said to me, "Well, Mum thought she'd dreamt the whole thing somehow." Let's be honest here, the whole scenario seemed like a dream to me. The following night I was sitting downstairs on my own again crying and asking him where he was. I kept saying out loud, "Where are you Daddy, are you all right? I just need to know that you're okay?"

I've got to be honest with you all, a part of me thought that I had somehow dreamt the whole of the previous night's experience and that somehow I had imagined that my father had come to talk to me. That my grief had somehow played tricks with my mind because even though I knew I could hear spirit voices there was no way that my father would have come to talk with me because of that damn gulf. Yet I desperately wanted to hear his voice again. And then to my complete joy he answered me. Again, I could hear his voice so clearly.

What was happening to me was beyond my wildest dreams.

God bless you Daddy a thousand times over. You weren't in the ground yet. We hadn't had your funeral and there you were talking to me and reassuring me. How blessed was I? How fantastic that I could hear him so clearly. But what amazed me the most was that my father was such a good communicator.

Someone once told me that love builds the bridge between this world and the next. Well if that was the case I could easily understand how we could talk to each other because there was so much love between us. He said to me, "I knew you would be able to hear me because I realised you were hearing voices years ago and I knew you would write my words down for me."

"But where are you Daddy?"

"Get your pad of paper I have something for you."

And here are the wonderful words that he sent me that night in March 1988.

The Colours

The grass is green much greener
than the brightest green you know
the colours are more vivid
than a picture postcard shows

You ask me to describe to you
the colours that I see
have you ever seen the colour blue?
more deeper than the sea

A rose so perfect one would think
the painter's brush you'd missed
gardenia and petunia and begonia stand in line
the colours of the rainbow
there that describes it fine

I'll give this garden all the love
I gave to mine on earth
I'm happy just to potter on
and sit and watch the earth

Now don't be sad
your eyes are filling up with tears I see
you should be very happy
because you... can hear... from me.

Let me be very honest with you all. I cannot read this to this day without crying my eyes out. Thirty years on and the tears are streaming down my face as I'm writing it, it's still so special to me. In a few simple words my father was able to portray to me exactly where he was. No, he hadn't suddenly sprouted wings when he passed over four days earlier, and no he hadn't been changed, he was still just my Dad. He was always good with words when he was here on this planet. After all he had his sermons to write and they were always worth listening to. So he had had thirty five years to practice his preaching and practice his writing skills and he was skillful without a doubt.

The next three poems that he dictated to me (all within the first week after he passed over) were for me alone and as you read them you will begin to see the gentle way in which he told me he was going to send me a book to write - all this before his funeral.

My Dearest Love

My dearest love
your friend in life
I knew you at your worst
yet all the time I knew your worth
was hidden from all sight

Your heart is great your love is strong
your faith will see you through
this strength will be a comfort
both to others and to you

You've built your life upon a rock
a rock that will not move
blessed is this rock you stand upon
for it reaches far beyond

You hear my voice you know it's me
I love you more each day
as your life goes on
your strength will guide and keep those
along the way

I love you dearly as I know your love
for me was true
no father could ever want
a daughter more precious than you

Keep to your faith
your heart is true
keep listening to your voices
you reach up high reach higher still
the doors will all be opened
but try and remember those simple souls
that need pulling even higher

*Look after all I cannot reach
their hearts are still not opened.
just call my name and I will be
by you ever more.*

Pages of Love

Take a pen and write the words I say
for I have great words to convey

I'm feeling I must write it all
and make my message clear

Be patient don't push your life
each step has purpose on your path

Learn from mistakes that you have made
remember memory doesn't fade

Don't carry anyone along
contrite I know
but they are weak and you are strong

Take courage that each step you take
you take with others near

So near that you would be amazed
but I know this isn't clear

It will become a task to you
as others will find strength
from being near and close to you
take heart your life's not spent

Great strength will come for you alone
to help you on your way

Be patient child - and you will receive
many blessings on your way

A book I'll give for you to print
a book of love and hope

Be sure it's used for everyone
be sure it's used with love.

The Book

Words of assurance
and comfort and love
have come tumbling from Heaven
all sent is pure love

To give us the message
to make it quite clear
when this life is over
in Heaven we'll be.

Perhaps the first line of this poem should be the title for this book because all the words that fill my somewhat battered silver file are all 'Words of Assurance' without a shadow of doubt.

Little did I know that this would be the start of me writing spirit messages not only from my father but from many other dear Souls.

CHAPTER FIVE

WONDERMENT

I now had five poems that I could take to my mother for her to read the next time I was due to visit her, but I decided in my limited wisdom at the time to only take two of them, because I had no idea how she was going to respond or react to everything that was being sent to me. The fact that I was telling her that I could hear my father's voice so clearly was as if I had suddenly learnt to speak a foreign language without anyone teaching me how. This was strange and shaky ground that I was walking on. This was all a bit alien to me, never mind my mum. I am saying this because the fact I could hear my father's voice was a miracle beyond miracles for me. I could tell you stories from my childhood where my father had been so against anything to do with spiritualism, but here was my father talking to me from - let's be a bit spooky - the grave. None of you will ever realise just how alien this was for my mother and how amazing beyond words this was for me. I might as well have landed a spaceship in her front garden and told her we were going for a ride. That's how alien this all was to her.

She had been taught and had believed all her life that there was a vast gulf between Heaven and earth and no one, and I do mean no one, could ever cross over it.

No one, absolutely no one.

So how the heck was I hearing my 'dead' father's voice?

Poor Mum.

I decided to take the letter that Dad had written especially for her for her to keep and a copy of the poem he wrote for me. But I would leave the other poems at home for another time. Mum sat with me and read them both over and over. Then she looked up at me from the pages she was holding, and said, "They really are from your father aren't they?" "Yes Mum they really are."

58

Mum then told me that she had been writing something herself.

"I've been sitting for the last few days worrying that I won't recognise him when it's my time to go Isabella, so I've written a letter to Billy Graham."

Now just in case some of you have no idea who this Billy Graham was, he was a very well known and respected American Evangelist at the time. He was a very charismatic and powerful preacher. I had gone with my mother and father to hear him preach when he had visited England in the 1960's not long after the Aberfan disaster had happened in Wales, in 1966. So I knew who she meant when she said she had written to him. Mum showed me the letter. It was about four pages long. Poor Mum was worried about so many things. From worrying that she wouldn't be able to find her way to heaven, to not being able to find my father when she got there and if she did manage to find him would he recognise her and she him? Would he even remember her? What if she couldn't find him, would someone be able to help her? Would she be able to see and hear like she could here on earth? Would she be able to find her mother and father? And on and on went her list of questions and worries. And when I sat and thought about it afterwards they are probably the exact same worries that many other people have who are left here on earth when a loved one leaves them and passes into the Spirit world, in other words 'dies'.

After I had read her letter I said to her, "Look Mum, why don't you wait a few days and see if Dad can answer your questions for you, he may be able to help?"

"Do you think so?"

"Yes Mum I do. Let's give Dad a chance Mum. You've seen what he has managed to write so far, so let's both wait and see if he has anything more to tell us."

(Bless her, she said she would.)

This was all so incredibly hard for her to comprehend. From being a child she had been taught by her parents that death is final, that there is no communication between heaven and earth. But there she was sitting holding her letter in her hand saying: "This really is from your father."

That very same night after my family had all gone to bed I was sitting downstairs on my own, but this time I was actually waiting for dad to come to me and it didn't take him long, just a matter of seconds. I asked him if he knew about the letter mum had written to Billy Graham? Dad said he did and he had already prepared an answer for her. As I was sitting all ready to write with my pad and pencil my father started to dictate his words to me. Oh boy - I could hardly write his words down through my tears. The words that he was sending were so beautiful and so meaningful. He was answering all my mother's questions in the most wonderful way imaginable.

This particular poem is over two pages long and over the years has become a firm favourite with many of my friends. It gives me great pleasure to be putting it in a book at long last. I'm so excited to be able to write this most fantastic story down once more and pass it on.

Please read it very carefully. Please read it very slowly. And as you read it, please take in every word he has written, because he explains himself so beautifully.

Wonderment

How can I begin to tell
the mysteries I have seen
the wonder of a magic land
and everywhere I've been

I must begin on passing
so beautiful and sweet
when the Angels gathered round me
for my life's work was complete

I felt no pain or sorrow
to leave the world behind
just a sudden thought on leaving
then I rose up high to find

I just floated like a cloud on wind
I felt so light and new
my body felt so wonderful
and fresh as morning dew

So many came to greet me
so many I can't tell
it seemed a thousand smiling wonders
gathered round to swell

The music, I could hear
the sound of Angels singing sweet
so many wonders I could see and hear
a world complete

I felt so whole my body new
as if by a magic wand
but the magic of our maker
is far greater and more grand

I try to explain the wonderment
but earthly words are poor
to describe the heavens mighty throng
the sounds so true and pure

You ask me why I feel no sorrow
I cannot shed a tear
I know your suffering down on earth
this to me is very clear

My spirit has moved on up high
I cannot interfere
for God's law of things is his alone
this you know is clear

My soul is on another plane
it's journey now complete
I'll wait for you until the day
our hearts as one will beat

You will know me I will know you
of this be very sure
God's law is love
no earthly thing will you find in store

Our love will be as souls entwined
never to part again
but you must rise above all else
and find your soul again

You lost it's love you lost all sight
with dogma and with pride
shed off this load you carry
let tears flow don't hide

The Lord will take your burdens
just leave them at his door
don't take them back and hide them
to add to your great store

Each person has a path to walk
each path alone must take
by you keeping to yourself
the cares of others you will break

You must let each life run for bad or worse
the choice is not for you
yes, give a helping hand to those
a helping hand will do

Give love and comfort where you can
but problems - they're not for you
you will affect the mighty plan
if you try and take them too
just let each soul make it's own way
and God will see them through

You see we each choose our own path
some rocky and up-hill
but this is ours alone to take
you see we have a will

You made the choice you chose your path
now lift your head up high
for your home to come is with me
in this wonder
way up high.

My mother was overjoyed when I was able to give it to her.

She sat quietly reading through his words very slowly, twice, and then without a word (I can still picture her as she did this) she got up from her seat and went to find her handbag. Mum pulled out the stamped addressed envelope she had ready to send to Billy Graham and with a smile on her face she tore the letter up. As she said there was no need to send it now because Dad had answered all of her questions in the most wonderful way imaginable.

She did ask me if I knew what he meant by the words in the verse beginning 'The lord will take your burdens' I smiled at her and said, "Yes Mum I think I do. I know you say your prayers every night before you go to bed asking God for help with all sorts of things and I also know that within minutes of you finishing asking for his help you start to worry about everything all over again. Think about it Mum, it's a bit like you've got your prayers on your knicker elastic."

"Isabella."

With a smile on my face I said to her, "Think about it Mum, imagine your prayers going up to heaven and St Peter is at the pearly gates waiting for you to finish so that he can take hold of your prayers and pass them on to God, and just as he's about to hand them over they disappear out of his hand and bounce back down to earth just as if they were on elastic tied to you. You no sooner ask God for help, than you take your requests back again and again and again. They are tied to your knicker elastic mum."

She burst out laughing.

"You're right"

"I know I am"

And we both started to laugh.

"Just leave them mum and stop worrying and give God a chance to help you. That's what Dad means."

"Okay Isabella, I will."

CHAPTER SIX

AND THE WORDS KEPT COMING

As you can imagine I was overjoyed by the fact my father was coming to me most nights to dictate to me more of his wonderful words. I was missing him so much it hurt, but the fact I knew he was very near me was a comfort beyond words. Only my husband, our two children, my mother my sister and my close friend Jean knew about the poems to begin with.

I'm not sure what our children thought or how they felt about their mum hearing their grandfather's voice at the time, but it didn't take them very long to ask if Grandad could please send them each a poem and of course he did.

A few years earlier, our son Alexander had spent a few hours on his own with his grandfather. The pair of them went fishing together while our daughter Marie and I stayed with my mum in their beautiful garden sunning ourselves and just having a nice quiet afternoon. When it got to tea time and the pair of them still had not appeared we all began to worry a little, but we didn't need to. When they did both eventually arrive back our son was beaming from ear to ear. They had been having such a wonderful afternoon together they hadn't realised what the time was and Alexander's very large smile was because he'd caught his first fish with his grandfather's help. My father told me afterwards that he had been amazed at how patient Alexander had been, because he was only about eight years old at the time. He apparently had sat very quietly by my father's side for hours waiting for the fish to bite, as they both sat and talked softly, so as not to disturb the fish. It was obvious to all that they had had a great day, one of those special days that they would both remember always. So here is the poem that my father sent my son some four years later.

Dear Alexander

The message that I send
is especially for you
I'm sending it across all time
with love and comfort to

The day we spent, meant more to me
than you will ever know
because we shared some space in time
I will remember you

Your young in years
you have a lot to learn my little friend
take comfort from the faith you have
for it will see you through

And as each day goes by in life
and troubles come your way
take heart - you do not walk alone
I'm just a step away

Do not be sad
I'm in our Lords most glorious land of joy
someday I'll come to greet you
one day - when you're a full grown man.

Needless to say, he was delighted.

Not long after my father passed over our son asked if he could have his grandfather's fishing lines and basket that was full of his fishing gear including a very old sweetie tin full of his homemade special flies that he used when he went fly fishing. When I asked my mother if he could have Dad's fishing gear she said my brother wanted it, but she would ask him if perhaps Alexander could have one or two things. My brother kept his best rod but allowed Alexander to have his old rods and yes he got the basket full of very special goodies and that was really what Alexander had wanted more than anything because my father had spent that special afternoon with him showing him how he made a 'fly' as they waited for the fish to bite.

About six weeks after granddad had sent the first poem to him it was Alexander's twelfth birthday and without him asking Grandad sent him a birthday message. Reading the next few poems you can see the different way in which my father's approach changed towards our son, as he grew into a young man.

Happy Birthday Alexander

You haven't yet gone fishing
with my line and basket yet
please take along my jacket
it might stop you getting wet

Get dad to organize you both
and when you both take part
remember I'll be with you
to watch and play my part

Just because I'm not down there
to go along with you
I'll be watching just the same
and I'll help in what you do

Listen for my voice
when you're casting in the line
and you will be amazed at what you catch
remember, that's my line.

A year went by with me writing Dad's words down nearly every night and then came Alexander's thirteenth birthday and this is what his grandfather sent him. It's almost priceless.

Happy Birthday

You've used my line my basket too
my jacket fits you fine
but your expertise is lacking
for the fish to hook the line

Don't give up and don't stop trying
for the skill will come in time
and the fish will take your bait
they might even break the line

You're growing son in stature
but you must not change your heart
for you've always known that love wins through
it can mend both limb and heart

Next time you take my tackle
ask me to come with you
just say to your self...I'm going
Grandad please come too

And as you cast my line in
think of me standing near
I'll be right beside you son
and there will be fish for tea.

A few weeks later Alexander went fishing with his father and guess what? We had fresh fish for tea that day courtesy of Alexander and his grandfather of course.

The following year on his fourteenth birthday this is what my father sent him.

Alexander

The time has come again to write
and wish you happy days
a birthday greeting sent to you
with love in many ways

Your fourteenth year a boy no more
a young man now appearing
your smiling face your laughing voice
makes people feel like cheering

I know this might sound daft to you
but as the years pass by
you'll realise what laughter does-
it lifts a soul so high

It helps each one around you feel
much brighter deep inside
keep smiling son
and lift those souls for God is on your side

I know I've said to Marie
how wondrously she's grown
but you've surpassed my greatest wish
as your journey starts back home

What can I say what words to give
a teenage youth like you
I love you Alexander, you're not too big
to send a hug to you.

Happy Birthday

My father in life was not a tall man.

In his youth (by all the pictures I have of him) he was quite handsome, and he kept his youthful good looks and his boyish smile well into his sixties, with a full head of hair and hardly any grey, but at a guess he was probably only about five feet four or five inches tall. Yet he had a presence about him, when he spoke people listened, when he walked into a room people would turn their heads. His aura shone out and that's what made people notice him.

Our son on the other hand just kept on growing. He was over six feet when he was in his early teens and when he wore shoes with a thick sole it made him even taller. Now a grown man he is six feet three in his stocking feet. I'm telling you this because of the words in the next poem my father sent him. This time my father's words are priceless. Absolutely perfect for a fifteen year old very tall young man.

Alexander

If I were to stand beside you
trying desperately to stretch
I might be very lucky
to come half way up your chest

I always knew you'd grow son
but when I look down and see
you're growing like a plant son
or should I say a tree

You know I'm only joking
but my words just half in jest
I'm really very proud son
even though your socks my vest

If your feet should grow much bigger
and your toes should sprout some more
I just thought that I could use them
perhaps a spade better still a floor

I know you'll grow still taller
may your heart and Soul keep pace
for then the love you'll have son
will be mighty for your race

Use the knowledge that you have son
use your faith in God above
for I love you still and always
you're my very special boy
Grandson.

Happy Birthday

CHAPTER SEVEN

FOR MARIE

It was right for me to record our son's messages first because he was the first person after my mum to ask for some words from Heaven, followed within a week or two by our daughter. So I'll go with the family theme for one more chapter and share with you the wonderful, and again humorous, words that her grandfather sent her.

Our daughter was my parents' first grandchild and my father adored her when she first came along.

When our daughter started to talk, one of the first words she said (apart from no) was Pompar. She couldn't say Grandpa, it came out Pompar. My father loved it and this is the first poem he sent her.

For Marie

I watched you as a baby
suckling at the breast
the first few words you tried to say
Pompar was the best

I do not think I heard you cry
not once in all the years
a happier lovelier baby
full of laughter and no fears

I watched you grow
and hoped and prayed
that you would turn out strong
with a loving caring nature
and to know what's right from wrong

I didn't need to worry
when I looked down from my place
for the love that has been given you
is written in your face

You've grown so tall
and straight and true
from that small baby that I
loved and knew

A woman now with strengths and fears
with human weaknesses and tears
do not let your heart be sad and down
just call on my love I'll be around

God loves you, just as I have done
so lean on him, His will be done

He sent that poem to her when she was fourteen years old. Then this is the birthday poem she received from her Pompar on her fifteenth birthday.

To my Dear Grandchild on Your Birthday

For Marie

Young lady how you've grown my child
from that little tiny babe
that I cuddled when you first were born
and worried for your days

My very first grandchild to hold
my very first to love
such a tiny little treasure
such a very precious babe

But when I look at you full grown
I marvel at the way
you've come together wondrously
our Lord I give full praise

Fifteen where did they go
the years that have fled by
I know I'm not down there with you
but I'm walking by your side

You're wanting to grow up so fast
you want your life your way
but please remember my grandchild
that life has many lessons on the way

And even when you're fifty
I know it's a long way off
you'll still be learning lessons
as we all do as we pass

Pass through this life of learning
to be kind unselfish too
and remember to be gentle
to all other souls like you

You are my precious grandchild
and I love you as you are
and I'll guard and guide and help you
till you reach your home afar

Happy birthday Marie
happy birthday child
may the Lord I love protect you
and his angels from afar

I will sing you happy Birthday
may your heart be full of joy
for I love you and I'm singing
sweet fifteen my love you are.

Love Pompar

Ah, that's lovely.

Then the following year, on her sixteenth birthday, this is what he sent her. And I must be honest, I love this one.

Marie

A birthday rhyme I send to you
my precious little one
a rhyme of laughter fun and joy
I send to you this day

A Birthday wish
as you blow out the candles on your cake
remember sixteen I was
a special time and place

A time in life when childhood's past
a time to think and pray
a time when all your longings rise
a time for you your day

Where have you been my little one?
what steps ahead to take
the world is at your feet today
my promise will not brake

The song was sung in your Mum's day
the words they still ring true
and as I remember I'll sing these words to you

Today's the day I've waited for
because you're not a baby any more
you've turned into the prettiest girl
I've ever seen
happy birthday sweet sixteen.

Now this next poem that he dictated for Marie is my favourite without a doubt. This is the one for me that is priceless.

Seventeen

Driving down the street one day
I chanced to spy a car
it looked a bit like Bunter's bike
large wheels, big lights, no bar

It's colours could not be missed by night
it shone just like a star
and who should I see behind the wheel
well - who would shout - 'Pompar'

It rattled and it banged along
no wonder people fled
they jumped onto the pavement
they could see the big red L

I stopped much too amazed by half
to see my precious girl
behind a wheel with L plates
my how the years have flown

If I could wish a car for you
I'd wish for something grand
four wheels, two seats, perhaps a floor
and oh yes a starting hand

I don't suppose you remember
or perhaps you haven't seen
but my first car was started
by a handle near the wheel

Have one great fantastic day
don't dunch the van to much
remember that I love you
that I love you very much.

CHAPTER EIGHT

ON THE LOSS OF LOVED ONES

When we lose someone we care about, no matter who we are, their passing causes us all to stop and think, think about all sorts of things.

The next few poems that I'm going to share with you are all to do with how we may feel after we lose a loved one. Let's be honest, most people find themselves with regrets and for some people 'a passing' brings a lot of fear to the forefront of their minds.

Perhaps I was just lucky, or perhaps you would say I was fortunate, because after my father died I had absolutely no regrets. That was a blessing for me. If you are one of the many (just like my mother was) that is still confused and down with so many questions running around in your head after losing someone you love, I hope the following poems my father scribed may be able to give you some comfort.

Show Your Love

We say if only we had said
the words our hearts felt deep inside
if only we could turn the clock
and say the words we always hide

If we could just be given
a second chance at life
then maybe we would open up
and give ourselves a greater chance

When dear ones friends and family
pass from us here on earth
it seems the same words echo
around and round the earth

We could have said, "I love you"
we could have said, "I care"
we could have filled the last few days
with love and not despair

If you feel your stomach churn
and empty deep inside
because you didn't say the words
that would have helped give peace inside

Be sure your loved one knows it now
and you must learn from life
that feelings hidden deep inside
give only pain and strife

Your loved one has forgiven you
do not rebuke yourself
forgiveness starts with loving
so start to love yourself.

To Greet The Dawn

If a loved one has just left you
and you feel alone and sad
and your thoughts are full of yesterdays
the good times and the bad

Sometimes our minds play tricks with us
and good things disappear
we catch glimpses of the bad
with all the worries and the fears

Our strengths are at their lowest ebb
we seem to have no fight
and as darkness spreads around us
we even fear the night

To overcome this feeling
on our own would be a task
yet the answer is quite simple
all we have to do is ask

Ask a power that when its source is tapped
will flood you full of warmth
and drive away all fears
of yesterdays bad thoughts

It will fill you with a feeling
of comfort and a calm
that will carry you through the dark days
until you come out to greet the dawn.

The Door

Death is but a doorway
an entrance very near
it comes to all who dwell on earth
yet to some it brings great fear

Why is it that, you're frightened
to walk through this door to peace
is it because you have no faith
and you think your life will cease

Believe me when I tell you
you are made of many forms
you have your earthly body
that holds your soul apart

This life is but a moment
when compared to time and space
a passing place of learning
to help your run your race

If you do not understand
the words I've written down
it's just because you haven't found
life's meaning, so profound

You're here to make a journey
of finding who you are
to find the inner part of you
that's travelled - oh so far

You have travelled down from Heaven
yes, you were there before you came
to walk this life was your choice
don't look for someone else to blame

You needed to learn lessons
you wanted to move on
and the only way to raise yourself
was in this earthly form

If that doorway still holds fears for you
that you'll disappear from sight
it simply means you've yet to find
your soul's eternal light

But when you do your path will be
alighted by your Soul
and you will know you've found the door
that will lead you right back home.

CHAPTER NINE

SMILES

During the first few months after Dad passed over he kept me very busy in the evenings as he dictated his wonderful words to me and I would like to share some of my own personal favourites with you now. They always put a smile on my face when I read them, and with a bit of luck they will do the same for you.

I can still remember exactly where I was when I sat and wrote the following words down.

It was one of those beautiful warm, still, summer nights. In fact it was so warm I was sitting outside in our garden in the twilight dressed in the sun dress I had worn all day. I didn't even need a cardigan on. I had gone outside with my pad of paper and a pencil thinking I might perhaps sit and write a few words down. As I was sitting taking in the night time fragrances coming from all the flowers in our garden, I can clearly remember saying to my father.

"Come on Daddy give me some words on this magical night?" And bless him, he did. And the poems you are about to read next, are the words he sent me.

A Garden

Have you ever walked a garden
in the stillness of the night?
has the quiet peace and beauty
touched your soul one summer night?

As the soft breeze brushes past you
whispering gently lightly felt
has the silence soothed your long day?
did you feel your body light

If you stop one summer's evening
from your routine toil and stress
and you take a walk outside yourself
for some inner peace and rest

You may begin to wonder
as your eyes are drawn up high
at the beauty and the grandeur
at the stars that fill the sky

Could an earthly hand create this scene
or has nature played a trick?
no friend what you see and feel
is God, His glory fixed.

Higher Ground

Just a tiny stirring
just a whispered voice
just a sense of peace and calm
when the Lord - He walks about

Can you hear soft voices
tinkling on the wind
or a passing thought in moment
or the flap of silvery wings

Let your mind be clear and peaceful
and you may hear the sound
of the Lords voice calling to you
trying to lift you to higher ground

Should you catch a glimpse of moonbeams
when the night is dark and still
it could be you saw a fleeting glance
of the pathway up the hill

There are many paths to heaven
some are long and some are short
but which ever path you choose to take
be careful how you walk

Don't try to find an easy way
for there is no such thing
you must be guided by your thoughts
these will take you on your way

And when at last you reach the top
and glory shines around
be thankful that you found the path
the path, to Higher Ground.

I absolutely love the poem you have just read.

I love the verse that says.

"There are many paths to heaven some are long and some are short, but which ever path you choose take, be careful how you walk."

Oh boy how true those words are. Whatever your religious beliefs, try always to be kind, learn to forgive and try to be generous, especially with your time. I promise it won't cost you anything.

Sparkling Ground

Watching the sun set
on a still summers night
one's mind can imagine
it's fancy in flight

As the wisps of the clouds
turn from crimson to gold
I can see streets before me
all paved with pure gold

As the colours start changing
from gold hue's to reds
then rubies start sparkling
as the road rounds the bend

As the hue's start to deepen
the blues that surround
I catch glimpses of sapphire's
on the gold sparkling ground

Is it just flights of fancy
is my mind playing tricks
or was it a vision
if it was, I'm transfixed.

This Glorious Land

What a glorious land of love and joy
of peace and laughter too

Where everyone is smiling
and everything is new

No sorrow and no suffering
is ever to be found

Just love in great abundance
in this - our Saviours land.

God Forgives

Does it matter if we falter
does it matter if we stray
will we still reach our destination
if we stumble along the way

If we give in to temptation
or reject what we've been taught
will this all be held against us
when we stand up to report

Will the Angels that are watching
as we walk along in life
be ready to condemn us
do we run away with fright

Now - let's stop and think a moment
let us ponder on these words
no greater love hath no man
than He sent unto us His Son

Would a God so great and mighty
with a love so pure and true
not forgive us if we slip a bit
because we do as humans do

Thank Him for He can see us
as we can not see ourselves
He can look into our inner thoughts
where He alone can dwell

He will know if you ask forgiveness
and will give a helping hand
to make sure your destination
is His home in Bu-le-land.

Heavens Glory

The roads are paved with sunshine
the mountains and the streams
they glisten with the love of God
as if the Lord could rain

His blessings touch on everything
from tree tops to the earth
each flower that grows gives off a scent
so sweet it could cover the earth

The colours are so deep and true
no colours have you seen
that could ever be as near to this
the colours that I've seen

The power of love is greater
than any evil deed
no evil could or can exist with this love
so super human and serene

Just think of something happy
just think of something good
just think of something wonderful
and multiply ten fold

And even then the majesty
of this great and glorious place
won't come anywhere within your grasp
heavens mighty and oh so wonderful place.

CHAPTER TEN

A VERY SPECIAL LADY

This is exciting for me. I have waited thirty one years to bring this poem to the attention of you all. So for me to say I'm excited is a massive understatement.

My mother once told me she thought I was the most patient person she had ever met, perhaps she was right. Perhaps I am patient; thirty one years patient.

And this is the story, as I wrote it in my first book.

Not only was I hearing my father's voice so clearly at night, I was also hearing other voices.

This was very confusing for me, because most of the time I didn't know who the voices belonged to. I could easily distinguish between male and female, but I was finding the whole experience a bit disconcerting. My father's voice was a wonderful comfort to me, but strange voices, I wasn't so sure.

I happened to be out shopping the day after one of my nightly events when I passed a bookshop and before I knew what I was doing I found myself inside without knowing why? It was as if I had been guided by unseen hands. My *voice* directed me through the shop straight to a shelf full of Mind Body Spirit books. I was then directed to look down at the books on the bottom shelf. And there on the shelf right in front of my eyes was a little book with the title 'Voices in my Ear' by Doris Stokes. I couldn't believe it. This was me, voices in my ear. Without hesitating I picked the little book up, took it to the cash desk, paid for it and left the shop smiling from ear to ear. I couldn't wait to get home to read it.

But of course the family came first.

As soon as everyone had gone to bed that night I started to read it. It made me laugh and it made me cry. I loved the way she wrote.

I was sitting on the settee saying out loud to myself "I

wish I could have met you Doris" when I clearly heard a woman's voice answer me back. (Crumbs.)

The voice said "It's me."

"Who?" said I.

"Doris."

Was I going bonkers or what?

"It really is Doris dear," was her reply.

I had said I was going bonkers out loud, but I don't think it would have made any difference whatsoever. She would have heard me anyway. Doris came to visit me for the next few nights as I read her first book. She was such a help to me. I'd never read anything like it before. She explained bits of her story as I was reading it. She was so gentle and kind.

Doris helped me to understand that hearing voices was no big deal, just a very natural thing. She said to me I should be really pleased that I could hear so clearly and not to ever be frightened or worried by it.

What a lovely Soul.

Not only did she help me, on the very last night as I sat and finished reading her first book she said to me, "I've got something for you."

"For me?"

"Yes, for you. Go and get your pad of paper and a pencil and I'll give it to you."

And that's when Doris dictated the following beautiful poem to me. She gave me the title; "A playground far from earth," and then she dictated the words that follow.

It's so precious.

I thanked her numerous times for helping me, not least for the wonderful gift of her poem and then she was gone.

Bless you Doris, wherever you are now.

And now after thirty one years these are the wonderful words that she gave me that night in August 1988.

A Playground Far Form Earth

The hardest thing in life
a mother has to face
is when a child she bears and loves
is taken from it's place

No one can know the feeling
the grief, the hurt, the pain
that little life has passed from us
and we can't take the strain

Our world has gone - it's empty
all love has slipped away
we seem to face a bleakness
that nothing will shift away

Yet - this child we loved is near us
so near and yet so far
just a step away from seeing
this may seem painful yet how far

No one can die for trying
these words that made me smile
still have that special meaning
from here on the other side

Each baby that comes to us
a short term spent on earth
is treasured and made happy
in a playground far from earth

No grazed knees or bruised elbows
or tears are here with them
just happy lovely laughter
from the many tiny bairns

Put all your sorrow from you
for your children grow each day
in a world so full of caring
that a mother would be proud to say

My child is in a treasured land
so safe and well looked after
how could I wish my child away
from the happy, for ever after.

I sat that night after she left me with the above words and cried.

I had only just read in her book how she lost her own son at the age of two. If my memory is correct she tells the story of how her child had been unwell for a little while and on this particular night her father came to visit her from the spirit world just a few days before her child passed over. Her father told her he would be coming for her son to take him home to Heaven. I can't begin to imagine the fear that must have hit the pit of her stomach as her father was telling her what was going to happen, or the overwhelming sense of foreboding she must have experienced knowing that her son was going to be taken from her, taken from this world. And then when her father did come for him, she describes in her book how her father put both his arms out to take her son from her as she was nursing him in her arms. Oh boy, I don't think my brain computed this at the time and it still can't. If my father had come to me and told me he was coming for my son when he was two years old, it would have broken my heart. Yet, somehow Doris was able to go on with her life. So the words in Doris's poem are even more powerful when you know her story. She herself lost her child. To me this makes the words that she sent all of us that much more special.

So please, go back and read the poem again, knowing what you know now.

Bless you Doris and thank you.

CHAPTER ELEVEN

MORE FROM THE SPIRIT WORLD

One particular night many years ago, I was sitting doing some paper work with papers strewn all over the coffee table in front of me with our local radio station on (tuned to a phone-in program). People would ring in and chat about anything they wanted to. I wasn't taking very much notice, but it kept me company, providing background chatter and some light music, while I was working. I was only half aware of a lady talking to the radio host about her recent bereavement. She was explaining all about it to the listeners, but as I said, I wasn't really listening when a lady's voice in my ear kept saying to me.

"That's my daughter, that's my daughter."

This voice wasn't going to go away.

By the time I had put two and two together the lady caller on the radio had finished telling her sad tale and I had no idea what on earth had just been said. I had to stop what I was doing and put my paperwork to one side because this voice in my ear was very persistent.

She kept saying to me.

"I have a message for my daughter. You must write it down and give it to her."

As I had a pencil and paper, I was able to scribe her message straight away. When I had finished writing it for her I just sat and cried when I read the words she had sent.

Now what was I going to do? I had been in a similar position once before but at least the last time I was able to find the correct address and deliver it to the family in person (even though I made a very quick exit after handing it over!), but this was not quite the same.

As I was going to see my mother the following night I had a thought. I'll show Mum what I had written and ask her what she thinks I should do with it.

When I arrived the following evening I explained what had happened the night before and I showed Mum the message. She cried when she read it.

"You must somehow pass this on if you can Isabella. Why don't you ring into the radio station and explain to them that you have a message for the lady who was so upset about two nights ago, they may be able to help."

Trust me on this one. If you had known my mother this would have been the last thing you would have expected her to have said. She was a very reserved, very old-fashioned lady.

This was not the response I had expected, but it was the response I needed to hear.

"You're right Mum, if this is meant to get to the right person it will."

If anyone of you out there still thinks I may have an ego forget it! I was so unsure of myself (still am most of the time). These are not the actions or thoughts of someone full of themselves they are the actions of a woman who thinks she may be wrong and doesn't like to intrude into anyone's life.

There was nothing for it, I was going to have to ring the radio station.

When I got home that night I waited until the same program was on air at about the same time of night and I rang the radio phone line. I asked the receptionist if she could remember the lady in question, she said she could. She told me she knew the lady's name and phone number but obviously she couldn't give the information to me. But she promised me she would ring the lady and let her know that I had a message to pass onto her. I hadn't told the receptionist what the message was or who it was from, just that I had one.

Four nights went by and no phone call came. Now what was I to do?

The voice in my ear had not gone away, it was still telling me to please pass on the message.

There was nothing for it. I was going to have to go onto the radio phone in program and hope and pray that the lady in question would be listening. I was going to have to read it out over the air waves. This now seemed the only way I could deliver the message.

Back to the telephone, the same phone in program, at the same time of night, I rang the telephone number.

The lady receptionist had remembered that I had rang a few days earlier so this time I explained to her that I would like to read the message that I had for the lady over the airwaves in the hope that she would hear it as she hadn't rang me. (The receptionist assured me that the program had passed my message on but obviously I had had no response.)

If you could have seen me, my legs were knocking together I was so nervous, but there was nothing for it, I had to pass this message on no matter what. Then a recorded voice said you are the next to speak live on air. I took a deep breath and prayed I would be able to read it without making any mistakes.

The radio host asked me what I would like to talk about so I explained to him that I had a message for the lady who had rang into the show about a week previously after her mother had died.

He said "Yes I remember, that was Edna, she is a regular on my show. What's the message?"

After I had finished reading it he said, "that was lovely."

I said goodbye and put the phone down.

Well, I'd done it now, no going back.

About three minutes later our telephone rang.

It must have been about two o'clock in the morning, I just prayed it wouldn't wake the family up, but it hadn't. When I answered the phone a female voice said, "please read the poem to me again."

Then she asked again.

She actually asked me to read it to her about five times before she explained the whole sad story to me.

Apparently, her mother had been ill for a long time and she had been looking after her, but in the process she had made herself ill. Her doctor had told her that if she didn't take at least a week's holiday herself to rest and recharge her batteries she was heading for a breakdown and then she would not be able to look after her mother. She reluctantly agreed to go away for a few days with her husband.

The sad thing was she went away on a Friday and her mother died on the Saturday. She said she would never be able to forgive herself for leaving her mother. She could not forgive herself for not being with her when she died.

So that's what the message was all about. Her mother was telling her from the other side of life that she had nothing to feel guilty about. She must have thanked me at least half a dozen times for passing on her mother's message.

I promised her I would put the message into the post for her the next day if she would give me her address which of course she did.

I must be honest and say I was pleased that I had taken the time to help. Very little effort on my part had meant such a lot to someone else. Thank you to the Universe for allowing me to help a complete stranger, in such a very simple way.

Edna's mother never gave me her name so I can't say a personal thank you to her but I can, of course, ask the Spirit world to pass on both my thanks and love (because they will know who she is). You did an amazing job of getting your words to your daughter and wonderful words they truly are.

For Edna

Just because you were not there
to hold my hand and smile
just because you were not there
when my spirit rose up high

Just because you didn't get the
chance to say good bye.
you mustn't feel you let me down
or spoilt our last goodbye

You were always there beside me
to help my feeble frame
you were always there beside me
through my needing and my pain

You were there for me with comfort
you were there and always knew
that I loved you for your helping
in my long life we both knew

Now stop this silly nonsense
and clear your mind of shame
just because you took a break
for your tiring caring frame

I will always think with kindness
of your loves unselfish deeds
and will try to help and guide you
through this trying time in need

Believe me when I tell you
you should be proud of how you coped
because you gave me all you could
your love, life's most precious gift.

CHAPTER TWELVE

AND THEY KEPT COMING

The next message – poem - I would like to record was from a very young lady, actually a distant relative of mine. Although I think the family will still completely disown me. They did at the time and I have no reason to think their opinion of me will have changed over the years. Nevermind. I said at the time this all happened, "I can't win them all."

In the summer of 1989 my mother told me about a family tragedy that had just happened. I hardly knew the relative involved but I had met some of the family many years earlier when as a child I was taken to a family wedding. My mother attended the funeral along with her cousin but I didn't go because I hadn't known the family personally. It was about a week later at my 'witching hour' while I was trying to work I heard a young girl's clear, bright and very cheerful voice speaking to me. I instinctively knew who it was.

She dictated a beautiful, very descriptive and happy message in poem form for me to send to her mother and father.

She explained to me that she was the teenage daughter of a cousin of my mother's and she was out for a walk with a friend when a car knocked her down. The emergency services and her parents had been called. As the accident had happened quite close to where her parents lived they had been able to get to the scene almost as fast as the ambulance. She had still been alive when her parents and the ambulance got to her but she told me she died soon afterwards at the roadside.

Her words told her story of what happened. Not the accident itself but how she had stood outside of herself watching the paramedics trying to revive her. How she saw her parents arrive at the scene and she had tried to speak to them, to let them know that she was okay. But of course they couldn't hear her.

Well, I had been here a few times before, so the next time I went to my mother's I showed her the poem and she agreed it was lovely and should be sent. She gave me the relatives' name and address so that I could send it to them in the hope that it would bring them some comfort in their time of sorrow.

I sat and wrote them a long letter explaining to them how I had been hearing from my father. How he had sent me, my mother and other family members some wonderful words of comfort when we needed it. Then I explained that I had also been hearing from other Souls. I tried to explain all of this in the hope that it would help them understand how I had been able to hear their beloved daughter's voice and dictate her words for them.

We all know in this life we can't win them all.

The response to my letter and the enclosed poem was horrendous.

My mother received a visit from her cousin about four days after I had sent the letter. She told my mother that the family had been in touch with her and they were furious with me. How dare I send them a poem supposedly from their daughter, their daughter was dead. I was cruel and obviously not right in the head.

I felt sick when my mother related this to me:

"You shouldn't have sent it Isabella, you really shouldn't."

"But Mum, you were the one to give me their address. I don't think it was our choice to make. Their daughter would not have given me the words if she hadn't wanted it to be passed on, surely?"

"You've got to stop doing this Isabella."

I was very confused and very hurt.

All I had tried to do was help.

All I kept thinking was I hope and pray they don't tear it up and throw it away. In the years to come they may come to understand and realise that it really was from their daughter.

For the next few weeks I tried to ignore any voices in my ear other than my father's, there was no way I ever wanted to be told that I 'wasn't right in the head' and that I was 'cruel'.

It was probably about three months after this that my mother said to me. "I've been thinking about the poem you wrote, I think you were right to send it. It wasn't for you or me to decide not to give it to the family. So I don't think you did anything wrong."

Now she tells me!

From a Lovely Young Lady for Her Parents

Hi Mam
hi Dad
it's really me
I'm writing this with help
Granda is by my side
and lots more are here to help

I want to say that I'm okay
I really am you two
I'm not in pain of any sort
you were there when I came through

I seemed to float outside myself
I didn't feel a thing
I saw you all so clearly
but I couldn't speak to you

I tried to tell you
I'm up here
but I didn't understand
then Granda was beside me
and he took me by the hand

He led me to a garden
so bright and full of love
it was then I realised
that I'd left the world I knew

I'm safe - I know you're crying
it's hard for you to know
that where I am is wonderful
and I can watch all you do

Please Dad don't blame anyone
it was time for me to leave
I'm trying very hard to explain
so you'll all believe

I'm here
I'm safe and happy
I can come and walk with you
and watch and learn to help
in all the things you do

Whenever I thought of dying
when I was a little girl
I thought of ghosts as spooky things
not something bright and new

If only people realised
what a wonder was in store
then no-one would be frightened
and death would be a door

A door that leads to wonderland
a place so bright and new
you must thank all the people here
who've helped to guide me through

I didn't write this all myself
it's all so new to me
but I'll be with you
and you'll know
this is really just from me.

I Love You All....

When our loved ones not only take the time but also find the energy they need to be able to communicate with us, to me it's very important that we take the time to thank them, and make sure they know that we appreciate their efforts. Such a shame this family did neither.

Not long after my father passed over I employed a new cleaning lady, she was a gem. We affectionately called her Mrs T. I would come home at tea time from the office to freshly cut flowers from our garden and a lovely smell of cooking coming from the kitchen. She was worth her weight in gold to me because she took a load off my shoulders.

My business was growing rapidly, and knowing there was someone at home doing the cleaning and occasionally preparing our evening meal was a Godsend to me.

Most evenings I would have paperwork to do after the family had gone to bed. I loved the peace and quiet in our home late at night, for me it was the perfect time to do my work, but many a night just as I was about to start my paperwork, either Dad would drop in to say hello or give me a poem to dictate, or some other Soul would want me to write something for a loved one. So it was no surprise to me when Mrs T's son dropped in with a message for her one night. It turned out that he had passed over about fifteen months earlier, just before Guy Fawkes Night.

Again, I was a bit apprehensive about giving her the message, but I was beginning to learn that if a person from the spirit world could somehow find the right energy to communicate with me here on earth, the least I could do was to pass the message on. It wasn't for me to decide who should receive a message and who shouldn't. So I gave it to her when I came home from work that next day.

She sat and read the message. She was quiet for a few moments and then she began to cry.

She had been with me for quite a few months when this happened but she had never told me what had happened to her son. This message was an opening for her to be able to tell me her own sad tale. Apparently her son, who had been in his late twenties when he passed over, had been at home alone watching television. He had been drinking from a can of beer and eating pizza all at the same time when he choked on his food and died.

All I could say to her when she told me her sad story was, "I am so sorry". After I had listened to her story I gave her a cuddle and then I explained to her that I had been writing messages from the Spirit world since my father had passed over. She was very pleased that I had received one for her.

And this is the message he sent her.

For Mam

Gone so quickly from this life
I was helped and shown the way
it seemed that I was just the same
still me I felt no pain

My guide was with me instantly
it was like a magic trick
I felt myself rise in the air
I thought I was on a trip

You know Mam I never ever tried
to experiment with drugs
yet the thoughts that were passing through my mind
were of excitement not of dread

I've passed now from the world you know
to another time and space
and I can see you grieving
from the world that's now my place

Please don't be sad
I know you think I'm gone for good from you
I'm not, it's just the path I walk
runs parallel with you

Just wait awhile
and give me time to learn the things I must
I'm feeling quite amazed
that this message can get across

I always thought that when you died
things came to a final end
how wrong I was, this is from me
Your loving son your friend

And as I learn to understand
the laws of Gods great love
my spirit will be strengthened
and in time I'll visit you

You will not see my spirit
but you'll know when I'm about
you'll feel my love around you
as you go about your house

Now come on Mam stop crying
dry your tears up now
your life is for the living
and I'm living by your side.

To a dear friend from her Son.

But that wasn't the only poem that her son managed to send.

The following year, just before Guy Fawkes Night, he sent his mother another message. And here are the lovely words that he gave me, to give to her.

Mam

The stage of life
I played it well
even though my part was small
and of all the players in my life
you were the most important one of all

You taught me from a little boy
to know what friendship meant
and to listen and to care for all
until my life was spent

I often come and watch you
as you work and rest and sleep
yet I can't get through your barriers
even when you're most relaxed, asleep

A year has gone now
in your world
a year so hard for you
yet for me it's been a miracle
the things I've learned to do

I've travelled far across your world
I've seen such marvellous sights
I still can't quite get the hang of it
this instant travel and flight

I gain in strength and wisdom
as each of your months go by
and very soon I'll have the strength
to open up your eyes

Your trying much too hard to hear
it's easy when you learn
just think of me just as I was
and picture me your son

I'm okay Mam you've heard these words
I'll say them once again
I'll also say I love you Mam
you're the greatest, I'm your friend.

Love Paul...

CHAPTER THIRTEEN

FOR YOU MUM

Now I could keep going with messages for people from their loved ones but I think this would be a good time for me to change track. I can always come back to more messages in a little while.

There is a poem I wrote in 1988 that keeps coming into my head and it won't go away so that's why I think now's the time for me to record it for you all. But before I can give you my words, I need to give you someone else's.

Let me explain.

If I sit and think about all of the poems I have scribed over the past thirty six years each and every one of them has had their own story to tell. The poem I would like to record now is no different.

My mother had sat and read me a story on one of the evenings that I went to visit with her after my father had passed this life.

She told me that she had had it in her possession for many years. I don't know who wrote it, because she didn't? And I don't know exactly how long she had been the keeper of it? But I could tell by the way she held the delicate pieces of paper in her hands and the light in her eyes as she read the words to me that it meant the world to her.

So, just for you Mum, with my love, I'm going to record it for you.

I have the ability now to do this for you, with love.

Then I will write down the words that came to me that very night when I got back home following her recital and her handing me the story that you are all about to read.

But for me to be able to write it down, I need to find it!

I have a feeling there will be a few of you reading this that won't be very happy with the words.

Why?

Because it's the life story of Christ.

But you all know my parents' history, so my mother was bound to have some religious writings in her possession.

I'm going to copy it down exactly as it was hand written, with all the 'odd' punctuation left in and I'm also going to ask my proofreader to do the same. I feel very strongly that no one should correct it in any way.

Please read it as if you were reading a story, because that's actually what it is.

I've taken a title from a very old hymn, as the story didn't have its own.

The Old Old Story

I'm going to read you a story
the story is about unseen things above
it's about Jesus and His glory
about Jesus and His love

And it must be the old old story
because this is the one I know to be true
and so this is the reason
I will read it now to you

Please listen while I read it to you
and may God help both you and me
to make this old old story
His message unto thee

Long long ago in Eden's Garden
God made and placed a happy pair
and all within was peaceful
till Satan entered there

Through him Gods word they disobeyed
the one thing to them he'd denied
they desired, they took they tasted
and that very moment, spiritually, they died

But in His love and pity
the Lord at once declared
how man tho' now lost and ruined
could after all be spared

Said God, the seed of the woman
would bruise the serpents head
and being a full salvation
and save them from the dead

Hundreds of years passed over
Adam and Eve had died
the following generation
and many more beside

At last some shepherds watching
over their flocks one night
were startled in the darkness
by a strange and Heavenly light

One of Gods chosen angels
had come from Heaven above
to tell the true true story
of Jesus and His love

He came to bring glad tidings
said He, you need not, you must not fear
for Christ, your new-born Saviour
lies in the village near

And many other angels
took up the story then
to God on High be glory
goodwill and peace to men

And was it true – that story?
they went at once to see
and found Him in a manger
and knew that it was Him

He whom the Father promised
so many ages past
had come to save poor sinners
yes, he had come at last

That was indeed His purpose
to seek and save the last
although He knew beforehand
knew all that it would cost

He lived a life most holy
His every thought was love
and every action showed it
to man and God above

His path in life was lonely
He was a working Man
who knows the poor mans trials
so well as The Saviour can!

His last three years were lovely
He could no more be hid
and time and strength would fail one
to tell all the good He did

He gave away no money
for He had none to give
but He had powers of healing
yes, even made dead people live

He did kind things so kindly
it seemed His hearts delight
to make poor people happy
from morning until night

He always seemed at leisure
for everyone that came
however tired or busy he was
they found Him just the same

He heard each tale of sorrow
with an attentive ear
and took away each burden
of suffering, sin, or fear

He was "The man of sorrows"
and when He gave relief
he gave it like a loved one
acquainted with the grief

Such was "The Man Christ Jesus"
the friend of sinful man
but hush, the story grows sadder
I'll read it, if I can

This gentle, Holy Saviour
without one spot or stain
by wicked hands was taken
and crucified and slain

Look! Look! If you can bear it
look at your dying Lord!
stand near The cross and watch Him
behold the Lamb of God

His hands and feet are pierced
He cannot hide his face
and cruel folk stand staring
in crowds, about the place

They laugh at Him, and mock Him
they tell Him to "come down"
and leave that cross of suffering
and change it for a crown

Why did He bear their mocking?
was He 'The Mighty God'
and could He have destroyed them
with one almighty word?

Yes, The Saviour could have done it;
but let me tell you why
He would not use His power
but chose to stay and die

You see, He had become our "Surety"
and what we could not pay
He paid instead and for us
on that most dreadful day

For our sins He suffered
for our sins He died
and not for ours only
but "all the world" beside

And now The Work is finished
the sinner's debt is paid!
because on Christ, The Righteous
the sin of all was laid

Oh wonderful redemption
God's remedy for sin
the door of Heaven is open
but only by faith you may enter in

For God released our "Surety"
to prove the work was done!
the resurrection of the Saviour
declared The Victory won.

And now He has ascended
and sits upon The Throne
to be a Prince and Saviour
and claim us for His own

But when He left His people
He promised them to send
the Comforter to teach them
and guide them to the end

And that same Holy Spirit
is with us to this day
and ready now to teach us
"the new and living way"

This then is "The Old Old Story"
oh will you take it in
this wonderful redemption
God's only remedy for sin

Do you at heart believe it
do you believe its true?
and meant for every sinner
and therefore meant for you

Then take this great Salvation
the Saviour Died to give
believe, and then receive it!
believe and you shall live

And if this "true true story"
has now brought peace to you
you make known "The old old story"
for other's need it too

Let everybody see it
that Christ has made you free
and if it sets them longing
just say, The Saviour died for me

Soon our eyes shall see Him
and in our Home above
we'll sing " The Old Old Story"
of Jesus and His Love.

There now Mum, it's done.

It's now recorded for all time, so if in the years to come your handwritten copy were to get lost or destroyed, the story will always be in print.

Writing this down has brought back many memories for me as I have been copying the words, not least the memory of the days I used to be brought home from school suffering from a migraine attack. Mum would help me get into bed and then she would go around the house doing her housework and she would sing. Sing loud enough for me to be able to hear her. She used to sing all the old hymns to help me to take my mind away from the pain I was in. And one of my favourites was a hymn called 'Tell me the Old Old Story.'

I haven't forgotten Mum.

Now the only reason I started down this avenue of thought was because of the words I wrote down when I got home after visiting Mum that night. My words 'kind of' follow on from the story she gave me. I use the words 'kind of' very loosely. But if I hadn't heard the story Mum gave me in the first place, I would never have written the following words down.

Heaven, Your Journey to Glory

Tonight I heard such a beautiful story
it told of our Lord
from His birth to His Glory
the words and the meaning
gave joy to my Soul
so marvellous a tale
wondrous story of old

May I now take my turn
with God's help and His guidance
to tell you a tale
one more wonderful story

This story to tell
is from way far beyond
I can't begin to explain
where the words all come from

Bear with me my friend
and forgive flowery words
but the wonder to tell
would lose meaning untold

I'll just let my pen flow
and with love in my heart
I will pray that the Lord
will great words there impart

I begin at the end
you may ask yourself why
it's all about Heaven
your home in the sky

We each ask ourselves
what will it be like
will we eat, will we sleep
even shoes on our feet

Our Lord told His Disciples
those Great men of old
there are many mansions
in my Father's House
I would have told you
if it was not so

What does this mean?
are there semis and flats
with great big stone pillars
and lines of detached

Or, was it symbolic
was the real meaning obscure
to our own earthly vision
can we make it all clear

Lord tell us about
your Great Home in the sky
forgive us for asking
but like children, we query
the reason, the why

Can our minds really take
such a wonderful concept
of places and marvels
our Souls one last conquest

Now Lord guide my hand
that the words that will follow
will be true and clear
for us on earth to follow

When over the bridge
from earth's realm you will pass
you will meet friends and loved ones
joyous meetings at least

Raise up your arms
and give praise loud and clear
you're free of all earth bonds
your road is now clear

You will wonder and marvel
at health all restored
such a glorious feeling
such a wonderful Lord

The road now before you
in Heaven my friend
on paths of pure sunshine
in Heaven - no rain

What a welcome you'll get
what a birthday surprise
when you find you can speak
you can walk, you can fly

Yes, you'll eat in abundance
and walks to enjoy
so make sure you are given
stout shoes to employ

Not that it matters
for no pain can exist
with this great, yes almighty
no sorrow, just bliss

There are homes by the thousands
just waiting for you
if in need of a rest
then just pull up a pew

How lighthearted this sounds
you may think – I'm not sure
if the words that are written
are true and are pure

Yet the fact you can grasp
every word written down
is a clear indication
truth – written down

There are cities in Heaven
nothing like those on earth
for they stretch far beyond
and encircle the earth

There are levels in Heaven
just like those on the earth
but the leader of Heaven
no comparison on earth

If you're happy to stay
in the home you will find
surrounded by loved ones
and content in your ground

Then be not disheartened
for that's where you'll stay
but you can if you choose
to reach higher each day

And if your Soul wishes
by learning and prayer
by Great Master's of time past
you can rise up in the air

To new homes of glory
But this time so much nearer
our Blessed Redeemer
our Master and Saviour

For the higher you rise
to the source of all light
you shed off all of your clothes
as it were — and take flight

To become — one with the Lord
what a marvellous journey
it begins
when you pass this life
and begin
your journey
To Glory.

When I sat and read the above words after I had finished writing them down that night I was amazed by the simple way 'Heaven' had been described to us all. And knowing what I know now, how very accurate the above words actually are.

Trust me - they are.

If by any chance one of you reading this has seen or read the poem that my mother gave me, please let me know. I would love to be able to find out where it originated from.

CHAPTER FOURTEEN

FOR MY MOTHER, FROM MY FATHER

I think now would be a good time to give you some of the beautiful words that my father sent my mother for some of her birthdays, and some of their wedding anniversaries. When I stop to think about all the wonderful words my father sent us all as a family, I don't think any of us actually stopped to think how fortunate we were at the time. I think when I'm finished, even you might say "gosh they are lovely."

After my father passed over, Mum tried her best to keep the garden around her home as neat and tidy as my father had kept it, but of course she found it hard work. I kept saying to her that Dad wouldn't mind if she didn't do it quite as well as he did, but no, she was going to do her utmost to keep it pristine, even if it caused her pain. So I wasn't surprised when Dad dictated the following poem to me for Mum.

Watching Over You

Watching from my place on high
looking down at you
working hard to keep our garden
clean and neat like new

Concerned that you might hurt your arm
by stretching as you toil
I sit and wonder at your strength
your inner strength the you

It's nice to see it looking neat
but don't try too hard for me
just potter round enjoy the peace
I'm watching patiently

You see the garden we have grown
now in your tender care
means little to a new born Soul
God's glory is so fair

I understand you want to know
if I think you're doing fine
of course I do but you mean more to me
then grass and plants that grow

Move on my love to pastures new
so that your toils are less
it matters not to leave behind
you need peace you most need rest

Dear blessed love I'm by your side
see me with strength renewed
I'm waiting I'll not move on
I'm waiting just for you.

It wasn't many months after Dad sent her the above poem that my mother decided to sell the bungalow that had been my parents' retirement home. She very sensibly decided to buy a two bed room, modern, sheltered-retirement flat, with a very tiny outside patio of her own where she could sit on sunny days, surrounded by a wall of pretty flowers. It took her all of ten minutes to water her little garden, just the right amount for her to tend to.

I love this next poem, sent to her for their 47th wedding anniversary.

As I was writing the words down as my father was giving them to me, he was painting such a clear picture. I could almost see them both as if it was their Wedding Day. For some reason, unknown to me my parents had no wedding photos. I know they got married during the war years and I know they had very little money, so they didn't have a big white wedding or a white wedding of any sort. I cannot believe I never asked my mother what sort of wedding day they had. I do have a lovely black and white photo of my parents when they were very young. Mum looks lovely on it and I have often wondered if perhaps that was taken on their wedding day. They both look so happy. Anyway, here are the words that he sent her on the 7th December 1988.

A Present From Heaven

What sort of present
what sort of gift
would I give you my sweetheart
to remember our bliss

Do you remember the day
that we both said our vows
to love and to cherish
through life's ups and its downs

I remember you know
that the day was so cold
and you worried and fretted
that we all would catch cold

So many years have gone by
since that day
yet I still can remember
my words and my prayers

That the Lord be beside us
in all that would come
and bless us and keep us
till our lives would be done

I can't be beside you
in flesh as you know
but I can in the spirit
our Lord has renewed

May the blessings of Heaven
pour down on your soul
and give you the warmth
in your heart from my soul

My gift to you Dear
from my place on my plane
is the knowledge and comfort
you will see me again

The Lord walked beside us
for all of those years
and kept us together
through comfort and tears

My prayers were all answered
47 years have now passed
and look at the memories
our children our past

It wasn't all easy
we both worked so hard
but the blessings our Saviour
gave us in our hearts
kept us together
through all of that time
and you're still mine my Darling
yes really just mine

Just look at the gifts you're
surrounded with now
our children all love you
and each other have found

You're still my Ma'Took
and on this special day
a present from heaven
has been sent just to say

I'm walking beside you
and I will all the days
till I'll guide you to Heaven
but my love till that day

Don't be downhearted
trust in our Lord
for treasures in Heaven
are awaiting untold.

I wonder if Mum every realised how blessed she was. How many women get a poem like that from their husband – nevermind the fact that he sent it to her after he died? Not many I'm sure!

I forgot to mention to you all that my father often called my mother 'Ma Took' or just 'Took.' Why or where this came from I have no idea but he used both these names with love. So for whatever reason they were his nickname for her. So this should help with the poem I'm going to include next. This poem wasn't just sent for Mum, it was sent to all the family exactly one year after he left us here on earth.

To My Family

What words of comfort can I give
to help you all today
because I'm not in flesh with you
I haven't gone away

I'm still so close, I see and feel
the sadness in your hearts
because I left you all behind
one year today apart

You've heard from me so many times
the words are written down
today I want you all to feel
God's love as it surrounds

Surrounds you all my family
and upholds you all with strength
to carry on as days go by
with dignity and strength

This love that holds you on your paths
is given to so few
a privilege from God's great store
is sent my loves to you

Each one of you must hold on tight
to each others love and care
a family my own to love
a family to share

My love is with you all this day
I'm especially close to you
may God grant that you all feel this love
it is sent to each of you

My love especially to Ma'Took
I bless you Annie dear
of the memories that trouble you
shed off and have no fear

I only feel as spirit can
a love so great and pure
your earthly tears for words once said
are earthbound thoughts and fears

And when you go to bed tonight
drift into blissful sleep
I'll come and walk with you awhile
you'll see me in your sleep

I'll walk with you and hold your hand
and tell you of the love
that God has granted to us all
that hold the Saviours love

His name is written on your head
the name of power and grace
and all your troubled thoughts tonight
with power He will erase.

Now back to Mum, this time for her 48th Wedding anniversary. I had great difficulty scribing their 47th anniversary poem down through my tears and I just know before I start that I'm going to have the same problem all over again.

My Darling Wife

My Darling wife this card I send
across all time and space
is sent with all my warmest love
from God's great home of grace

The year has gone for you so slow
yet time to me seems short
it only seems like yesterday
that I took you to my heart

Those carefree days those summer nights
when walks were all in vogue
I wonder now what youngsters do
to find their one true love

Another gift I send to you
a gift so clear and bright
that on the heavenly shores one day
our Souls will reunite

The sunsets of our bygone years
the laughter in your voice
will once again be heard by me
my one true love, my wife

My dearest love you walk with faith
you're blessed in many ways
our Lord will guard and guide you dear
until our happy day

And when that day shall come my love
your Soul will glory see
and I shall walk you there my love
forever in eternity to be.

Those words are beautiful.

The month of March became a very busy month for me. Mum's birthday, my birthday, Mother's day, the month my father passed over. Yes! a very busy four weeks for me.

Two Years Apart

To my wife and all my children
to the ones I hold so dear
to the little ones now growing
I am sending words of cheer

Two years have gone so quickly
two years of mixed up thoughts
for you all have different feelings
as your Souls have different thoughts

I have watched you all so closely
I am helping all I can
and the love I send to all of you
is sent from God's great hand

His hand can hold the world in
His hand can move the stars
yet this mighty hand will hold you all
with tenderness and calm

Your prayers are all being answered
though it might not seem to be
yet the world around you changes
and your lives so changed will be

I will always be around you
I am never very far
for I've still so much to pass to you
from God's great home afar

Your home to come is wondrous
no words can clearly tell
or describe to you the glory
where my Soul now lives and dwells

May the light that shines from heaven
reach you all to help this day
that your sorrow may be turned to joy
for my Soul is home to stay

You're my family and I love you all
stand firm and walk in faith
and one day we'll be united
for you have our Lord's great grace.

I've learnt such a lot myself over the past few years as I have been writing my stories down. I'm still not very good with the grammar side of things (where do the commas go, that's my worst problem). My spelling is not too bad because I have a spellchecker and, of course, if I'm not sure of a word I can always look it up on the web (or even a dictionary). Let's face it, the web is so much quicker these days. I can't believe how much I've been able to learn and take in. I have had to learn to use a computer and all that goes with it. From copying and pasting words and sometimes even pages of writing and the most important thing of all, remembering to keep saving what I have been writing. I once lost ten thousand words and I sat and cried. That wonderful man I call my husband somehow managed to find them for me and I've not lost a word since. I have since learnt to use a data stick. When I think back to my first days at school, I had a small slate black board and a bit of white chalk. Yes - all the children in the class had small chalk boards to write on. That's how we did our lessons and no, it wasn't the eighteen hundreds, it was the 1950s. And Dad, God bless him, was no different. He just got better at writing his poems as each year went by and the next two he sent mum will prove my point. They are both amazing. The first one is from December 1990 for their 49th wedding anniversary. And then the second one is from December 1991 for their Golden wedding. And I just know I will need my box of paper hankies right beside me as I try and copy them down for you all to read through my tears.

I think perhaps I should put a warning notice at the front of this book saying a box of paper hankies is a necessary requirement before you start reading.

My Dearest Love

I am coming down the pathway
to the gate of rustic truth
where our Souls shall meet rejoicing
meet me there
my own Ma Took

No more days of pain and sorrow
no more days of toil and stress
come my love and walk the pathway
home my love
to peace and rest

Hear me speak and know I'm with you
gently will I call to you
softly will the cord be broken
then my love
our joys made new

Celebration preparation garlands made
in every hue
flowers that no earthly vision
could comprehend
are here for you

My joy at knowing you are coming
is almost more than I can bear
just because I'm here in spirit
does not stop
what you call care

Two years ago I sent a present
to reassure you of my love
to confirm, that yes you'll know me
but much more
you'll know our love

One year ago I talked of glory
Walking with you hand in hand
the time is nigh to walk beside you
Annie dearest, the promised land.

Golden

I am standing right beside you
with my hand held tight in yours
just like I did my sweetheart
50 years ago

It's still our day my treasure
and as I've said before
may we give our Lord full praise
for my voice can still be heard

Just know that I am with you
that I'm with you all the way
on this our anniversary
on our very special day

Golden are the rays of love
that gently fall to you
golden is the colour
for gold is strong and true

Golden days ahead my love
to share on golden shores
I'll hold your hand again my love
my gold with me once more

Golden is the colour
of the gates that you will pass
golden that is how I'll feel
when I have you home at last

Golden, what a wondrous word
it speaks of precious things
it best describes the way you are
come home on golden wings.

Amazing. I almost want to end this book on that note, "come home, on golden wings."

My father would have won a poetry writing competition with both of those poems, they are so beautiful.

If any husband were to write those words to any wife; we would all be very happy girls.

CHAPTER FIFTEEN

PRAYERS

Quite a few of the poems my father sent me during the late 1980s could be described as prayers. They could and can be used by anyone who needs a bit of extra help and guidance.

A Simple Prayer

Just a simple prayer tonight
to send you on your way
from one who loves you dearly
this message is to say

Sleep tight sleep sound
sleep in great peace
your heavenly father watches you
you're in His might keep.

Another simple prayer

*Go to bed
and rest your head
and let your body fall
into the arms of God's great love
awaiting when you fall.*

God's Gifts

Oh the bright and glorious sunshine
of a dawn so clear and true
makes the earth a shimmering yellow
In the early morning dew

As the birds all rise to take the air
their songs ring out to say
God's gifts renew the earth each day
as His love replenished you.

Safe Home

Wherever you are
wherever you may be
may the lord bless and keep you
and bring you safe home to me.

Imagine

Abide with me and call my name
and as you fall asleep
imagine me beside you child
I'll walk with you in sleep.

Rest on the Arms of Jesus

Rest on the arms of Jesus
rest in His loving care
rest in the safe assurance
Jesus is everywhere

Sleep in the safe knowledge
sleep in comfort - not despair
for the Lord will watch and keep you
while you sleep in His tender care

Rest your head on your pillow
sink into His love
leave all care and worries
because you're safe in Jesus love.

A Prayer to Hold

Oh wondrous source of peace and love
oh wondrous source of life
I pray your grace will fill the years
with love for this Soul's life

Be near me Lord
and guide my path
that every step I take
be filled with goodness from the source
of peace and love and grace.

\

The prayer you have just read is my favourite of them all. I wanted some words to use each day before I started work, something to put me in the right space and energy and the above words were the words that were sent to me to use.

As with all the poems and prayers in this book if anyone needs to use them, use them with my love.

That's why all of them have been written – to share.

CHAPTER SIXTEEN

OUR THOUGHTS & SOMETIMES OUR FEARS

Our minds can get us in such a muddled, fearful state sometimes. Our fears surface from an unknown dark place and take us by surprise.

There are so many things in our lives that can cause this to happen. I'm not even going to try and list them. We all know what they are. Please read the following poems that Dad sent us all and let my father's words lift and comfort you.

Thoughts and Fears

Have you ever thought of Heaven
and got stuck quite soon in thought?
because our choice of words are small
our pictures all fall short

Now don't blame books or language
or any other source
how on earth can we place Heaven
in our mind's eye with our thoughts?

We try to picture something
that our minds can't comprehend
because you see we live on earth
not in celestial realms

Don't be bothered if you give up
with the pictures you have seen
just be sure that Heaven's glory
will far exceed your dreams.

Questions

Why is it that we don't believe
or understand in life
that we of so much learning
find simple things a plight

We ask ourselves great questions
so many it's untrue
these questions can't be answered
by me or even you

What purpose do we say
are we here at all on earth
what part to play and why
are the questions from our birth

Who do we think we are
to give the answers we may seek
can't we be satisfied
it's not for men to seek

Yes seek yourself keep searching
for the you to come quite clear
but leave the mighty questions
to one who knows and is very near

The Universe is infinite
your mind is small and weak
compared to the mighty presence
it's of the Great 'I AM' I speak

They say they will find the answer
to the creation of all time
don't be too sure of the answer
only God knows and he alone – in all time.

Sharing

If only everyone was honest
and said the things they keep inside
if only people would tell each other
of all the thoughts their minds keep and hide

If Souls could talk to one another
along life's highway on the earth
then nearly all the troubles round us
would cease and there'd be peace on earth

When you feel love for one another
give it freely ask no price
just share yourself and ask no favours
just like God's love it has no price.

Troubles Shared

Though the road seems long and weary
and the path seems long and hard
there is reason to be worried
if you do not share your load

We are given friends and family
to share our troubles with
for without them life is bleak on earth
and you will find no peace

We need to share life's troubles
for a trouble shared is halved
and the meaning may seem clearer
to another person's part

So if you have no family
or friends to share them with
then turn to those departed
because they still can be reached

Your answers may be jumbled
but if you give a listening ear
the answers to some questions
will become crystal clear

There's no one on earth today
who won't get comfort through
just ask for a helping hand
the comfort is for you.

The Road in Life

As the rain beats on the window pane
and the wind howls round the doors
do you feel yourself all shivery
or do you feel a special warmth?

When you walk along a lonely road
and mist is on the ground
do the hairs behind your neck stand up
or do you walk the road with calm

Do you lie in bed awake at night
and when you hear a creak
do you cuddle down beneath the clothes
or do you turn and go to sleep?

Is your mind so full of nervous thoughts
that your shadow could cause alarm
it's just because you've lost your way
from the source of peace and calm

As we walk along the road of life
we do not walk alone
we each have someone very near
to help and guide us home

Your fears are in your mind alone
your earthly mind, I mean
your Spirit is a separate part
the real you has no fears

Remember what a mighty Soul
said to his friends on earth
I'm with you to the end of time
I'm with you in your place

You never walk along alone in life
take comfort from these words
you're very special in your place
yourself is a mighty Soul.

CHAPTER SEVENTEEN

OUR HOME TO COME

I think I'm getting close to the end of this first book of poems, I say first because I do have enough for a second book! But just before I come to a close, I would like to leave you all with some uplifting words.

Words of Assurance

Words of assurance
and comfort and love
have come tumbling from Heaven
all sent in pure love

To give us the message
to make it quite clear
when this life is over
in Heaven we'll be.

This Glorious Land

What a glorious land of love and joy
of peace and laughter too

Where everyone is smiling
and everything is new

No sorrow and no suffering
is ever to be found

Just love in great abundance
in this – our Saviour's land.

Eyes

It has been said so many times
that failing eyes grow dim
they lose their sparkle and their light
as they grow dark with strain

Yet even when the curtain falls
and nothing can be viewed
our senses tell us day from night
and everything's the same

What splendour we can conjure up
what pictures we can see
and nothing can come between
these pictures so serene

No clouds can pass the sun's bright rays
no mountains can obscure
the heavenly sunset we can see
now that our vision's pure

The rainbow colours bright and true
can lift your soul up high
remember passing from this world
your eyes will be made new

And oh what joy tenfold will be
as bleak and dim no more
your eyes survey the wondrous scenes
restored to health once more.

Old Coat

When your bones all start to stiffen up
and movement makes you sore
and everything's an effort
walking's painful sitting more

Your feet feel full of stones and glass
and eyesight seems to dim
don't be worried by the body's signs
of old age though they may seem grim

You've had your share of healthy days
you ran you jumped and played
I'm sure your mind is very clear
of those bright and happy days

Just because your coat's all worn
and you feel trapped inside
you will be set so free and strong
you'll be amazed at your own prime

It won't be long now till the day
you'll rise and spring with ease
and you will feel the feelings
of those young and carefree days

Your old coat you will leave behind
and from its dusty cast
a magnificent and splendid robe
will you possess at last.

A Special Trip

If the sun was to shine
all the days of your life
and rain only fell
on the world in the night
and your garden was full
of delights to the eye
and your nose could pick rose scent
oh what splendour what joy

The sun that surrounds
in this home safe and sure
caresses the spirit with rays of pure joy
the air is so clear no horizon in sight
just wonderful colours
such a magnificent sight

If all of these wonders
on earth did appear
you would hide
for so awesome it all would appear

Tell all of your dear friends
to prepare for a trip
tell them no luggage allowed
just themselves for this trip

And when over the threshold
and into my land
what a marvel will greet them
our Lord's wonderland.

CHAPTER EIGHTEEN

THANKS DAD

The second last poem that I'm going to record for you was sent to me at the end of a very difficult time in our family's life and I can remember that it gave me a great deal of comfort.

I had been sitting one evening going over in my mind all the things that had been happening to us. I picked up my pencil and my pad of paper and just started to write.

The words just started to flow and this is what I wrote.

Our Daily Lives

When life seems to be too heavy
for our human hearts to bear
and the problems of our daily lives
like mountains in the air

What can we do what prayers to ask
what words will ease the pain
does God know about an overdraft?
can he understand our pain?

We tend to think the God of old
is far beyond our grasp
does he understand a mortgage
when the payments have elapsed?

Will the car be there tomorrow?
will the children's shoes last out?
can the milkman wait till next week?
does God know what life's about?

Does He sit serenely with a smile
with eyes of brilliant blue
with a long white beard like Santa Claus
on a shimmering cloud of dew?

Do the words that were recorded
by so many men of old
mean anything at all today
are prayers really heard above?

Has God watched all the seasons
has He seen the changes made
does He know the twentieth century
has a price that must be paid

Let's not think about great countries
let our minds not reach too far
we have got to sort our home life
and the principals so far

I don't think that He meant us
to be poor and badly dressed
or to worry or be saddened
by a life of stressfulness

Why is it that we're burdened
have we missed some major word
have the teachings that He sent us
gone by and not been heard

There have been great masters
in the art of writing words
and their gifts and inspiration
have all helped us down the years

Charles Wesley wrote some wondrous words
of faith and hope and cheer
so many years ago now
yet their meaning still rings clear

He took his words from scripture
with a faith beyond all price
for he knew this Lord and Master
would take our pain and strife

It could be you're thinking
that your creed is not of mine
and your customs and religion
don't correspond with mine

You may call your Lord and Master
by different word of speech
yet, we're told there is but one God
and one day our paths will meet

What did those men of old know
that their words were strong and sure
with a faith to move a mountain
for a loving God so pure

Has the twentieth century rat race
with its hassle and its haste
turned our hearts and minds to stone
is there time to walk in grace?

As I sit with pen and paper
in the stillness of the night
I'm sure our God in Heaven
guides my hand as I write

He wants me to tell you
in a simple humble way
that He understands our problems
and He hasn't gone away

As a child looks to its parents
for the things it needs in life
for warmth food and protection
and our love without a price

Perhaps the simple lesson
from a child can teach us much
is to trust our Heavenly Father
for the price was paid for us

A simple trust not complex
just believe that He is near
and will hear your prayers whenever
you can trust that He will hear

Just give the Lord your problems
make a list if this will help
and as you say them to Him
cross them off your list now spent

Just hand them to your Master
and when given leave them there
feel the burden lifted from you
and believe that God still cares

If you do this in spare moments
you will come to know like me
that our God above still loves me
twentieth century
it may be.

Wherever those words came from, or whoever gave me them to me, thank you.

I would like to leave you all now with one last prayer from my father.

The Lord be With You

May the Lord be with you in spirit
may He guide you and comfort your soul
may He hold you so tight in His presence
that you feel lifted and strength in your soul

Take His hand and feel lightness of spirit
heed His voice and your life will be held
in the strength of His love and compassion
for your soul is His only my friend

May the Lord give joy to your loved ones
may He fill you with life's only wish
that when passing from this world of sadness
you're surrounded with His love and His gifts.

CHAPTER NINETEEN

THE PERFECT ENDING

How many of us are blessed with more than one friend? Over the past fifty years I have been blessed to have a few very close friends and Jean will always be one of them, no matter how many years pass by without us seeing each other. She was the dear friend who was very much with me when my father passed over in 1988. She was the friend and confidant that I turned to when all sorts of strange and wonderful things began to happen to me, including my first healing experiences outside of my family circle.

When my writing journey began Jean told me about a poem that she had written in 1972 and I asked her at the time if I could please have a copy, which she gladly gave me. I have kept it safe for the past thirty years. It has always been at the back of my very full silver file of my father's (and Spirit friends') poems. So it's very fitting that Jean's poem is the very last poem to be written down in this my (our) first book of poems.

From Jean

Do I believe in God, I cannot guess
is the answer no, or is it yes
when I look into the skies
I find it rolls before my eyes
what is it lies behind those clouds
is it people dressed in milk white shrouds
who once were friends upon the earth
will they see another birth
or do they stay there forever
tasting God's celestial weather

If God himself could hear me now
would he stop and wonder how
my faith could be so poor and faint
do you think he'd send a Saint
to try and make me see the light
and do you think for me he'd fight
and do you think when he has won
that I shall see his heavenly Son
there to greet me when I die
I wonder if that time is nigh
will I look upon his face
and know that I have found the place
a place of peace and quiet there
a place where no one has a care

But then again I often wonder
when we finally come asunder
and death rolls back our waning eyes
don't you think we're in for a real surprise.

Printed in Great Britain
by Amazon